EMPOWERING KINGDOM GROWTH

TO THE
ENDS OF THE EARTH

EMPOWERING KINGDOM GROWTH

TO THE
ENDS OF THE EARTH

CHURCHES FULFILLING THE GREAT COMMISSION

JERRY RANKIN

Ten-digit ISBN: 0-8054-4425-4
Thirteen-digit ISBN: 978-0-8054-4425-4

Published by Broadman & Holman Publishers, Nashville, Tennessee
Hardback version (ISBN: 0-9767645-0-4) under same title available from the
International Mission Board by going to http://imb.org.

Dewey Decimal Classification: 266
Subject Heading: FOREIGN MISSIONS

Unless noted, Scripture quotations taken from the New American Standard
Bible®, Copyright © 1960, 1962, 1963, 1968, 1971, 1972, 1973, 1975, 1977, 1995
by The Lockman Foundation. Used by permission. (www.Lockman.org)

Lottie Moon Christmas Offering® and Annie Armstrong Easter Offering® are
registered trademarks of Woman's Missionary Union.

1 2 3 4 5 6 7 8 9 10   10 09 08 07 06

IN HONOR OF . . .

Thousands of missionaries who have served with the International Mission Board throughout its 160-year history, and have given their lives to plant the gospel and extend the kingdom of God to the ends of the earth;

Tens of thousands of short-term volunteers who go overseas at their own expense each year to work alongside missionaries, provide encouragement, and multiply the evangelistic impact on a lost world;

Southern Baptist churches that give faithfully and cooperatively through the Cooperative Program and Lottie Moon Christmas Offering® to support the work of the International Mission Board. They are discovering the joy of direct involvement in the global missions task.

Contents

PREFACE

God's concern is about His kingdom. He is the Creator and sovereign over the universe. He alone is worthy of all worship and praise and desires that all creation come under subjection to His Lordship and reign. Throughout the Bible we read of a coming kingdom of God where every tongue will confess Him as Lord and every knee will bow in humble submission to His power and authority. The Old Testament narrative tells how He chose a people to be His possession and commissioned them to declare His glory among the nations.

Jesus came announcing the arrival of that kingdom which would be purchased by His own blood upon the cross. He sent His followers to proclaim the gospel of the kingdom to the ends of the earth and to make disciples of all nations. In fact, in Matthew 24:14 He said, "This gospel of the kingdom shall be preached in the whole world as a testimony to all the nations, and then the end will come." All who come to Jesus Christ in personal repentance and faith become a part of that kingdom. And, as a kingdom people, we are to be the instruments for extending His kingdom and reign among all peoples.

The kingdom grows as we acknowledge the Lordship of Christ and allow His reign in our lives to impact our families, communities, society, and our nation. God is glorified when people recognize His authority, are obedient to His will, and live according to His Word. But there also is a sense in which the kingdom grows quantitatively and geographically. Jesus spoke of the kingdom as leaven, small and practically unseen, but permeating a whole loaf of bread. That is how we are to be in society—making an impact for righteousness on the whole. He also described the kingdom as a mustard seed—the smallest in the garden—which grows into a large tree.

The kingdom, which began with Jesus and His small band of disciples, is to grow until it encompasses the whole earth. His kingdom is to be inclusive of every tribe, language, culture, and nation. Therefore, we, as a kingdom people, are to actively and deliberately extend the kingdom through our witness and obedience to Christ. It is not Christian organizations, denominations, or mission agencies that extend the kingdom. Only through a massive grass-roots force of believers functioning as the church, the body of Christ in the world, can an impact be made on a lost world.

The Holy Spirit can empower the growth of the kingdom. But it is the role of the denomination at every level to empower churches in the sense of facilitating, equipping, and enabling them to fulfill God's purpose. The Southern Baptist Convention (SBC) has adopted a vision for "Empowering Kingdom Growth." It is a vision that is greater than church or denominational growth. It is bigger than our programs. It is a God-sized vision for impacting our world for Jesus Christ. Every SBC entity—whether an association, a state convention, or mission agency—exists only to serve, equip, and enable churches and the people of God to fulfill the Great Commission.

When people and churches are mobilized and equipped to be all they are divinely designed to be in society and the world, the result will be growth—kingdom growth. Our one desire should be to crown Jesus as Lord in our own lives so that He might become Lord of all nations and peoples for the glory of God. Just before Jesus departed to return to the Father following His death and resurrection, He gave a formula to His followers for how spreading the gospel was to happen. It is found in Acts 1:8. They were to plant the gospel in Jerusalem where they lived. It was to expand from that small mustard seed to permeate the surrounding province of Judea. Then they were to extend the kingdom cross-culturally to Samaria and from there to the remotest parts of the earth. That New Testament process now leaves us with the mandate to reach the whole world. The mandate in Acts 1:8 reflects a simultaneous process to witness where we live and among all peoples wherever they are, whether in our communities, states, nation, or overseas.

Our denomination is uniquely organized to facilitate that very pattern of kingdom growth. The cutting edge witness and building blocks of the kingdom are local churches. Associations have been organized by cooperating local churches to more effectively reach their "Jerusalem." State conventions exist to mobilize the efforts of churches collectively to impact their states or "Judea." The Southern Baptist Convention has organized the North American Mission Board (NAMB) to coordinate and empower churches to reach out beyond their own communities cross-culturally and geographically to extend the kingdom throughout the United States and Canada, or their "Samaria."

And the International Mission Board (IMB) exists to lead—mobilize, facilitate, and enable—every believer, every church, and every denominational entity to result in expanding kingdom growth to the ends of the earth. This book will describe the driving vision and passion of the IMB to see the Great Commission fulfilled and the kingdom of God extended among all peoples.

God is moving through global events in unprecedented ways to make that possible as we have moved into the twenty-first century. To stay up with all God is doing has required making fairly radical changes in organization, leadership, and strategy. That is not to reflect on those who have gone before. Indeed, leadership and strategies in each past generation have been effective. They have not only established the kingdom in many countries through a growing network of national churches, they also have laid the foundation for the current expansion we are seeing today.

It is because of the faithfulness of former missionaries and the effectiveness of mission strategies that we can seize the opportunity for even greater impact and more widespread kingdom growth today. In 1997 the International Mission Board adopted what came to be called "New Directions." It really wasn't new but represented a sharpened focus on what had always been our purpose. The intent was to position us for maximum global impact when we crossed the threshold into the twenty-first century four years later. Now identified as "Strategic Directions for the 21st Century" (SD21), these initiatives have resulted in greater advance in global evangelization than anyone could have imagined.

But with growth and increased opportunity came the realization that the task of international missions could not be done by missionaries alone and the limited resources of the International Mission Board. The Great Commission is the responsibility of every local church. We can cooperate in sending and supporting missionaries, but only as every church becomes involved in God's mission can the kingdom be extended to the ends of the earth. This realization has resulted in a new vision of mobilization and equipping the local church to reach the nations and peoples of the world. That is the theme of this book.

Beginning with the vision that drives us—a vision consistent with God's purpose, characterized by God's power, and compelled by God's passion—the reader will be confronted with the clear mandate of Scripture and needs of a lost world. A foundational prayer strategy and an unequivocal church-planting methodology will be seen as essential components for kingdom growth. Churches will find practical handles for participating in short-term volunteer projects, sending missionaries, adopting Unreached People Groups, providing cooperative support, and joining partnerships that expand our potential and accelerate the harvest.

It has been my desire for several years to produce a book such as this to serve as a tool for local churches. It is intended to provide an awareness of how God is at work throughout the world, an understanding of the strategy and work of the International Mission Board, and how churches can have ownership and participate in reaching the nations. I am grateful for the many IMB staff members and friends who provided inspiration and encouragement for this project, particularly Avery Willis, former Senior Vice President of Overseas Operations, and Larry Cox, former Vice President of Mobilization. Many IMB staff members and pastors of our partner churches read and critiqued the manuscript, offering constructive suggestions.

I am especially indebted to Scott Holste and the staff in our Global Research Department for providing data, statistics, and graphics. They monitored the accuracy of the material in order to accurately reflect what God is doing. Bill Bangham, former editor in chief of *The Commission* magazine and now our director of photography, invested a massive amount of time and effort in partnering with me to rewrite and organize the material. Anita Bowden, senior editor, applied her finely honed editorial skills to the draft, and Dan Allen, Media Group leader in our Office of Mobilization, managed the whole process, carrying the project through to publication. Countless others at the IMB have been a part of the process, contributing to content, design, and marketing efforts.

However, as we were preparing this book for publication, something happened that changed even my perspective on the urgency of our Acts 1:8 kingdom task. On December 26, 2004, an earthquake of phenomenal magnitude shook the Pacific Rim and South and Southeast Asia. The resulting tsunami swept the coastlines of eight Asian nations and as far as the African coast; more than 250,000 people died that day. The tragedy was personal and affected me deeply. I had served as a missionary in that part of the world for 23 years. I consider Indonesians "my" people. My family had vacationed in some of the resorts in South Thailand that were wiped out. I had traveled with national co-workers along the seaside roads and through the coastal villages in Sri Lanka where thousands lost their lives.

My horrified reaction to what I witnessed in the news, as the report of fatalities mounted, was grief, concern, and an administrative adrenaline rush to step up and do everything we could to respond to this situation. But later, as I got in touch with my feelings, I realized the emotion I was feeling was anger. I was angry that this many people were lost for eternity, and that most never had a chance to hear of God's love.

The media has quoted many as saying, "Where was God in all this?" The implication was that He was not all powerful, or, if so, was not the loving and caring God He should be to allow such a tragedy. But I think that is the wrong question. The question is not where was God, but where were we? Where were we when thousands of people were swept instantly into hell?

Have we allowed the resistant Buddhist faith of those in Thailand to create a lethargy and indifference about pushing the gospel to the edge there? Have we observed the rampant terrorist activity and Tamil-Sinhala warfare in Sri Lanka and said it's too dangerous, it's not worth the effort; we'll wait for things to settle down? Because foreigners and Christians have not been allowed in Aceh, Indonesia, have we just thrown up our hands and said there is nothing we can do?

Yes, I am angry that it is taking us so long to get the gospel to all peoples. I'm disappointed that we continue to give so much attention to maintaining and nurturing established work where the gospel is readily accessible; we prefer the gratifying harvest fields where we can bolster our egos with impressive statistics while millions of Acehnese, Sri Lankans, Maldivians, and Thais are swept into hell, untouched by the gospel. I'm exasperated that we continue to spend 97 percent of our resources in concentrating on our Jerusalem, Judea, and Samaria rather than moving out to reach the ends of the earth.

The world will not quickly forget the tragedy of more than a quarter of a million people being killed by the tsunami on December 26, 2004. But it is easy to ignore the fact that nearly that many people die every week—week after week—in South Asia alone. That many people die from AIDS every month in sub-Saharan Africa, most without having a chance to know Jesus. Yes, I know I will soon get over my anger and adjust to reality. We will move on, doing what we can. But I have prayed, "God, don't ever let me be satisfied with business as usual. Don't ever let me lose a sense of urgency for sharing the gospel with every nation, every people group, and every person."

All I could hear, as I thought of the people who died, was the cry of the disciples on that storm-tossed sea as they cried, "Carest thou not that we perish?" There was nothing we could have done to prevent the death and destruction created by that powerful tsunami, but we could have done something to prevent such a massive loss of souls for eternity. One day we will stand accountable before God for failing to reap the harvest where hearts were open and responsive. We will give an account for those who never had an opportunity to know Jesus. For God has committed to us the task of being His witnesses and discipling the nations. May we be found faithful as we empower the growth of His kingdom, literally to the ends of the earth.

CHAPTER ONE

KINGDOM GROWTH—
GOD'S PURPOSE, OUR VISION

IMB PURPOSE:
That all peoples may know Him.
IMB VISION:
We will lead Southern Baptists to be
on mission with God to bring
all the peoples of the world
to saving faith in Jesus Christ.

We had been driving for two hours and had long since left any semblance of what could be called a "highway" in Bangladesh. The bumpy, pothole-broken pavement of a secondary road that had not seen maintenance in many years had given way to a narrow, dirt road in which sharp curves became more frequent as we climbed into the hills. The crowds of pedestrians spilling onto the roadway, all with burdens on their backs and shoulders, had begun to thin. The snarl of ox carts, bicycles, and pedicabs had gradually diminished as we left the populated towns and markets behind us. The occasional open-bed trucks, straining in low gear with their loads of rice sacks capped with a mountain of hitchhikers perched precariously on top, had been sighted less frequently the farther we traveled into the countryside.

That day our travel left a cloud of billowing dust that caked the green vegetation on each side of the road with a layer of brown. A few months earlier during the monsoon rains, the road would have been impassable, even in our four-wheel-drive vehicle, as the rutted terrain would have been barely distinguishable from a free-flowing stream. For someone who had lived many years in the tropics, the ferns, palm trees, and thick foliage were nothing distinct; only the scarcity of people was noteworthy in a country where 140 million people live in an area the size of Arkansas. But someone unfamiliar with the region would have clearly noticed, probably with some anxiety, that we were in the midst of a jungle. Overhanging trees filtered out the sunlight. Vines wove the foliage into an interlocking barrier, isolating us from whatever might lie just a few yards beyond our vision. Monkeys would dash out of the roadway into the trees as we rounded a curve.

It was late summer of 1990, and I was accompanying R. T. Buckley, veteran missionary to Bangladesh, into a remote area of the country bordering Myanmar (formerly Burma) and northwest India. As we turned north into the Chittagong Hill Tracts, as the area was known, we had driven for several miles in view of the Indian border, just a few hundred yards to our right. R. T. had been asked by the Bangladesh mission to leave his assignment for a couple of months to probe this isolated region and assess potential response among a people group called the Tripera. Bangladeshi believers, who had encountered these people in the markets of nearby cities, had alerted missionaries to this massive population group that, as far as they could discern, had never been exposed to the gospel. R. T. had reluctantly agreed to the temporary assignment, although already overextended in administering relief among the destitute villagers in his area, supervising the drilling of water wells, training leaders, and nurturing disciples within the growing numbers of churches in his assigned district.

It was now almost two years later, and he was continuing to make trips into the area. Eleven churches already had been started, and baptized believers were gathering to worship in 14 other villages. When R. T. first entered the area, he found it was true that these people had never heard of Jesus. He related an experience on one of his initial trips to establish contacts with several villages. On his way home he saw two men running down a hillside onto the road, and he stopped his car. When he asked what they wanted, they said, "Are you the man who is telling about a religion that provides forgiveness for sin?" The message that R. T. had been preaching had been talked about and shared from village to village.

When we arrived at one of the villages, the elders and most of the men gathered to welcome us. As we received their hospitality and sipped steaming cups of tea, R. T. identified the two men he had encountered on the road. After telling them he had related that experience, I asked them, somewhat incredulously, "You mean you had never heard of Jesus or the Christian faith?" The two men and others affirmed they had never heard of such a religion, reinforcing the isolation of their environment. They knew about the Muslim religion of most of the people of Bangladesh and the practices of Hindus across the border in India, but they had never heard of Christianity.

Picking up on the story I had been told, I asked, "Why did you want to know about a religion that offers the forgiveness of sin?" I will never forget their response. Several began to talk at once saying they knew what sin was. They became drunk and abused their wives and children. They defrauded their neighbors. They continued to elaborate on the reprobate lives they had led. Then one of them, speaking on behalf of the group, said of their consciousness of sin, "And we knew it had something to do with what happened to us when we died!"

Seeking further understanding, I asked, "If you knew about sin, but did not know of God's forgiveness through Jesus Christ, what would you do about your sin?" The group became very animated, all talking at once, as they told of making clay images and praying to them, or putting offerings under a banyan tree where they perceived the spirits to be living. They continued, "But we never had any sense of peace or assurance that our sins were forgiven until we heard of a God who loved us and gave His Son as a sacrifice for our sins."

Since R. T. and his Bangladeshi co-workers were unable to visit these villages frequently and were limited in their access to this politically sensitive border area, I asked them how the Christian message was spreading so effectively. They explained that people from other villages came and asked why their village was now clean and why the people got along so well. It had been observed that they did not get drunk, they treated their wives with respect and were honest in their dealings. These new Christians then told them about Jesus and how He had changed their lives. As the trails converged from throughout the region into the valley, and these men went to work in the fields with those from other villages, they shared the joy of their faith and the difference it made.

As we visited throughout the afternoon, and I continued to hear testimony after testimony, a repetitive theme emerged—"It's just a matter of time until all the Tripera become Christians."

Recently R. T. and his wife, Fran, retired after 30 years in Bangladesh. I recalled this experience of 10 years earlier as they participated in an emeritus recognition service and asked him, "How many churches are there among the Tripera now?" He said it is really impossible to know since the villages are so remote and spread out, and it has not been possible for him as a foreigner to go into much of the area. "But," he said, "the church leaders tell me there are more than 120 churches and at least that many more among a neighboring tribal group among whom they had shared the gospel."

I've never forgotten the vision and faith of those new Christians among a remote tribal group in Bangladesh who were hearing the gospel for the first time. "It's just a matter of time until all the Tripera become Christian." They had experienced the life-changing power of the gospel and in their simple faith understood that this was what all people need and are looking for. They were demonstrating the reality of a living Savior, not just spreading the teaching that a missionary had brought to them. Their witness was not an effort to introduce a new religion into their culture but reflected evidence of changed lives. They became a living witness to the lost and those in darkness around them. I don't know if they were familiar with Romans 1:16, but they clearly reflected the conviction that, "The gospel is the power of God unto salvation to all who believe."

The vision the Tripera believers have for their people becoming Christians is a vision we should have for all the peoples of the world. It is a vision that grows out of the conviction regarding the power of God to change lives and evangelism to spread spontaneously beyond a missionary witness. It is such a vision of all peoples coming to faith in Jesus Christ that will motivate us in our mission task. An image of the future in which the kingdom of God is extended to the ends of the earth will keep us focused on activities that move toward that objective.

Without a vision, church programs and mission strategies can go in any direction. Organizations can define their purposes, identifying their objectives and goals, but it is a vision or image of the future that keeps us focused and on track. It is a vision that keeps us from being diverted to secondary or trivial activity. It is a vision that will enable an individual, a church, and a denomination to be effective in fulfilling God's kingdom purpose.

The word "vision" comes from the Latin, *spiare*, which means to breathe or to inspire and energize. Without a vision inspiring us, driving us, and energizing us, we tend to flounder and dissipate energy and resources, responding to pressures and going in multiple directions without really getting anywhere. Burt Nanus, in his book, *Visionary Leadership,* said, "There is no more powerful engine driving an organization toward excellence and long-range success than an attractive, worthwhile, and achievable vision of the future, widely shared."[1]

The IMB has always been guided by strategies or plans for evangelizing a lost world and fulfilling our Great Commission mandate. All missionaries and mission teams have strategies to accomplish their objectives and reach their particular assigned areas. But a strategy is only as good as the vision that drives it. My predecessors, presidents of what was then called the Foreign Mission Board, were all visionary leaders who challenged Southern Baptists toward greater goals.

Toward the end of World War II, M. Theron Rankin had a vision for mission advance and expanding our witness in a world that was suffering in the aftermath of global conflict. Baker James Cauthen rallied Southern Baptists with a vision of opening new fields and tripling the number of missionaries during his 25-year tenure. Keith Parks had a vision of focusing on the whole world and initiated innovative strategies to penetrate closed and restricted countries. All of those visions were largely successful, and the International Mission Board found itself facing the end of the twentieth century with an awareness that God was moving in unprecedented ways throughout our world.

Change was rampant as the Iron Curtain fell. The Soviet Union disintegrated and global alliances took new forms, opening doors for extending God's kingdom and mission advance. Communication and technology were bringing the world closer, but ethnic tensions and conflicts were tearing it apart. As we moved into the twenty-first century, responsiveness to the gospel reached dimensions that were unimaginable a few years earlier. The terrorist actions of September 11, 2001, as many have said, changed our world forever. Subsequently eight of our missionaries were martyred, victims of violent deaths within a time span of 15 months. Our sense of security has been shattered, international relations are strained, global economies are in disarray, and warfare against an elusive terrorist enemy appears to be here to stay.

There is no question that our world is changing, confronting us with new challenges in fulfilling God's kingdom purpose. Our society and our churches are changing. New opportunities for reaching a lost world are constantly emerging. But how does one adapt and change? We are seldom comfortable with change, but someone has observed that if the external changes exceed the internal changes of an organization, it is moving toward irrelevance and ineffectiveness. There is no question that our world is changing. Political upheaval, global relations, and international conflicts have resulted in greater sensitivity to spiritual needs and mission opportunities. Attitudes shaped by postmodern influences have impacted our churches and challenged traditional denominational programs. There is a tendency to react to the immediate, respond to the urgent or to hold on to the comfort and security of how we have always done things in the past. Only a vision can keep us focused on our kingdom task, put change in perspective, and keep us from being diverted from fulfilling God's purpose.

A VISION CONSISTENT WITH GOD'S PURPOSE

The vision that guides each individual who serves God must be shaped by a commitment to fulfilling God's will and purpose. Likewise, the vision that guides a church toward being a kingdom people in the world must be consistent with God's purpose. Like the gospel penetrating the Tripera and spilling over to neighboring tribal groups, it is God's purpose for all the world to have an opportunity to know and worship Him. The Bible clearly teaches us that it is just a matter of time until people from every tribe and language and nation come to saving faith in Jesus Christ. That is the vision of God's redemptive mission in sending Jesus Christ to die on the cross.

We often quote what may be the most familiar verse in the Bible: "For God so loved the world that He gave His only begotten Son, that whoever believes in Him shall not perish, but have eternal life" (John 3:16). That world is not just the world of our shopping malls, manicured lawns, and well-appointed offices in the communities where we live, but it includes all the peoples of the world. It includes people in dusty, remote villages in Africa where people are held in bondage to their charms and fetishes and where more than 6,000 die of AIDS every day. It includes more than a billion people in India, most of whom bow before lifeless Hindu idols in a futile search for blessings and enlightenment. It includes multitudes of Muslims across Northern Africa, the Middle East, and Central Asia declaring their belief in Allah and Muhammad as his prophet in a fatalistic faith that offers no hope and assurance.

The kingdom of God is the reign of Christ in our lives, our homes, our churches, our communities, and wherever He has been revealed. He blesses those who acknowledge His Lordship and give priority to glorifying Him. But Jesus also spoke of the kingdom in terms of quantitative and geographic growth. The kingdom parables acknowledge a small beginning, whether as leaven or a mustard seed, which would permeate the whole and result in phenomenal growth. He sent His disciples to proclaim "the gospel of the kingdom." That good news of God's redemptive love is an empowered message designed to extend the reign of Christ eventually to people of every tribe, language, and nation.

If we are to be a part of facilitating growth of the kingdom of God, we must seek to be involved in making Jesus Christ known among the nations. Our passion must be to see God glorified, not just in our own lives and in what we do, but among all peoples, even to the ends of the earth. A kingdom perspective is self-centered but with an outward focus. God has brought us into a relationship with Him, but the only justification for our existence as the church, as the people of God, is to facilitate building the kingdom of God through evangelism, discipleship, and missions.

We tend to have an egocentric theology. If most Christians were asked why Jesus died on the cross, they would reply, "To save me from my sin." That is correct; He did die for all. When we come to Jesus in repentance and faith, His death on the cross is for the penalty of our sins, and we are saved through faith. But note the answer to this question in the words of Jesus Himself as He explains to His disciples why He died on the cross. In Luke 24:46–47 Jesus said, "Thus it is written, that the Christ would suffer and rise again . . . that repentance for forgiveness of sins would be proclaimed in His name to all the nations, beginning from Jerusalem." His death wasn't just for us. It was to provide a message of forgiveness and salvation that is to be proclaimed among all nations.

Those nations are not the geographic, political units we know on our maps as countries but rather the multiplicity of culturally diverse language and ethnic people groups throughout the world. If there is Scripture every Southern Baptist knows, next to John 3:16, it is *the Great Commission* in Matthew 28:19–20. "Go therefore and make disciples of all the nations, baptizing them in the name of the Father, and the Son and the Holy Spirit; teaching them to observe all that I commanded you; and lo, I am with you always, even to the end of the age." The words that Jesus used which are translated *all the nations* in the original Greek are *panta ta ethne*, which literally means *all the peoples*."

That phrase may not seem to be grammatically correct, as the word *people* is already a plural noun. But Jesus is not talking about evangelizing all people, that is, all the individuals in the world, even though that would be His desire and bring glory to Him. The expression He used, *ethne* or *ethnos* is the same as our word ethnic, those distinct cultural and racial characteristics that distinguish some people from others. Rather, Jesus is commissioning His disciples—which includes us today —to bring into the kingdom of God and make disciples, Christ-like followers, of every ethnic, cultural, and language group in the world.

We have had a tendency to dilute the Great Commission to mean whatever we do in witnessing, evangelism, and ministry. However, there is only one active, transitive verb in this command of our Lord; all other verb forms—going, baptizing, teaching—are participles. But the imperative verb *make disciples* grammatically requires an object. In our English translations *disciples* appears to be the object of the verb *make*. In the Greek language, *make disciples* is one word; it is an imperative verb and the object is *all peoples*. The parallel passage in Acts 1:8 makes that responsibility clear whether the people group, language, and culture are in Jerusalem, Judea, Samaria, or at the ends of the earth.

It is only recently that we have come to understand our Great Commission task in terms of the peoples of the world. We used to think that sending missionaries to any given country would eventually evangelize an entire nation. Take Yugoslavia as an example. Events in recent years have shown us that Yugoslavia really wasn't a cohesive, homogeneous country. It is an area that consists of Serbs, Bosnians,

Croats, Slovenians, Kosovars, Macedonians, and other people groups. They have different languages and cultural identities. Conflicts in the region have been highlighted on our newscasts, and it is evident these people don't especially like one another. Penetrating one of these people groups with the gospel doesn't mean it is going to spread to others who speak different languages and have antagonistic relationships. Each one needs to be evangelized. Another example is the country of Pakistan. We are not sent to evangelize Pakistan but to make disciples, followers of Christ, among the Baluchi, the Punjabi, the Sindhi, and Pashto and other people groups who occupy the country.

We have discovered the world is not a pancake but a waffle. When you pour syrup on a pancake, it will flow all over a smooth, round surface, but not so with your waffle. It is a matrix of squares separated by ridges. If you want syrup all over your waffle, you have to very deliberately pour it into each little square. The world is not a monolithic collection of homogeneous peoples, like a pancake, but instead it is made up of more than 12,000 diverse languages, tribes, and ethnic identities. Like the ridges on a waffle, there are barriers that keep the gospel from flowing cross-culturally.

An obvious barrier is language differences. A research database known as ROPAL (Registry of Peoples and Languages) identifies 6,809 distinct languages. Only 2,322 of them have some portion of Scripture; fewer than a thousand have the full Bible in their language. Many of them are oral cultures and could not read the Bible even if one were available in their language, so illiteracy may be considered another barrier to fulfilling the Great Commission, due to our traditional methods of evangelism and discipleship.

Geography is a barrier as many people groups who have never heard the gospel are isolated, like the Tripera, in places where missionaries have never been allowed, primarily in the Muslim world or former communist countries. There is no church in their midst and no believers among them to be a witness. Totalitarian governments that prohibit religious freedom, or any expression of it whatsoever, are barriers to getting the gospel to all peoples. But whatever the distinction, cultural identity is a matter of "us" and "them"—those who belong due to common language, distinct values, and relationships in contrast with those who are outsiders. God's desire is that all the peoples of the world know Him and worship and exalt Him.

Due to accelerating evangelistic efforts in recent years, we are told that perhaps as many as 10 percent of the world's population—some 600 million—are now born again believers. When we think of one out of every 10 people having come to saving faith in Jesus Christ, the task of reaching everyone becomes doable; all it would take is every Christian winning nine. However, the problem is a matter of proportion. Unfortunately 95 percent of those believers are clumped together in America and other places where the church has been established, while hundreds of people groups, some numbering in the millions, have yet to hear the name of Jesus. Researchers estimate 1.65 billion people have no access to the gospel almost 2,000 years after Jesus sent His followers to make disciples of all nations.

God's heart and mission is that all peoples know Him, and our mission can be no less. The vision of our mission task must be consistent with God's purpose. It was the reason that He called Abraham to leave his home and family that "all the families of the earth will be blessed" (Genesis 12:3). The redemption that would be provided through Jesus Christ, the seed of Abraham, was to touch every nation, all peoples, and every family clan and tribal group. The Psalmist envisioned the time when, "All the ends of the earth will remember and turn to the Lord, and all the families of the nations will worship before You. For the kingdom is the Lord's, and He rules over the nations" (Psalm 22:27–28).

This is why God called Israel as His chosen people. In Psalm 67:1 they prayed, "God be gracious to us and bless us, and cause His face to shine upon us." We often quote this verse at the conclusion of our worship service as a benediction, say, "Amen," and go home. But the following verses read, "That Your way may be known on the earth, Your salvation among all nations. Let the peoples praise You, O God; let all the peoples praise You." The only reason God would choose to bless

Israel and favor them was so they would be His instruments to fulfill His purpose and make His way known throughout the earth. Why should we expect God to bless us and prosper our church programs if not for the sake of proclaiming His salvation among the nations, those peoples who live around us, and to the ends of the earth? God's desire is for all the peoples to know Him and praise Him. He is worthy of all honor and glory and praise, but He is being deprived of the praise of the people groups who do not yet know Him and have not yet come to faith in Jesus Christ.

One of the first passages of Scripture I remember learning as a child in Vacation Bible School was Psalm 100, which begins, "Make a joyful noise unto the Lord, all ye lands" (KJV). Psalm 96:1 says, "Sing to the Lord, all the earth." But how can that ultimate objective be realized in all the lands and all the earth praising His name? The answer is found in the next two verses. "Proclaim good tidings of His salvation from day to day. Tell of His glory among the nations, His wonderful deeds among all the peoples" (Psalm 96:2–3). That is clearly God's purpose from the foundation of the world. It was His purpose for His people throughout the Old Testament and was reinforced when Jesus, having purchased redemption for a lost world, sent us to be witnesses to the ends of the earth and to make disciples of all nations. We are constantly encouraged to be witnesses and lead people to salvation where we live, but tend to ignore the rest of this admonition of Scripture to proclaim God's wonderful deeds to all peoples. We are told of the power of the gospel in Romans 10:13, "Whoever will call on the name of the Lord will be saved." But then we are confronted with the question, "How then will they call on Him in whom they have not believed? How will they believe in Him whom they have not heard? And how will they hear without a preacher? How will they preach unless they are sent?" (Romans 10:14–15).

Often churches draw a circle around their community and see their mission simply as reaching the people where they live. Certainly God wants us to witness where we live and minister to the people around us, but if we don't carry the gospel to those who have never heard, who will? How can we expect people to confess Jesus as Lord in places where there are no churches to be a witness of the gospel if we consider ourselves and our church exempt from the task? God said to Israel in Isaiah 49:6, "'It is too small a thing that You should be My Servant to raise up the tribes of Jacob and to restore the preserved ones of Israel; I will also make You a light of the nations so that My salvation may reach to the end of the earth.'" God would say the same thing to us. It is too small and limited a task to just share the gospel among our own kind of people where we live. If the world is to know and worship Him, we are the ones who must proclaim the message and extend His kingdom. Because God has given us the privilege of knowing Him, we have a responsibility to share that with which we have been entrusted—the light of the gospel—with the nations, until news of His salvation literally reaches every people group to the ends of the earth.

Many churches have distorted their purpose as the people of God and have limited the scope of their responsibility. They reason, "We send and support missionaries to fulfill the Great Commission and reach the nations overseas." But it is not the responsibility of the International Mission Board to do missions on behalf of Southern Baptists; the Great Commission was given to every believer and every church. The role of the IMB as a denominational mission entity is to serve, enable, and facilitate all Southern Baptists to be obedient to God's kingdom purpose and fulfill the Great Commission. Our vision states, **"We will lead Southern Baptists to be on mission with God to bring all the peoples of the world to saving faith in Jesus Christ."** All peoples coming to faith in Jesus Christ is obviously God's desire and purpose, but that is not our mission; it is God's mission! "Missions" is the activity of God in the world through His people to fulfill His mission. And He is seeking to involve us in His mission and what He is doing in the world. Our vision is to "lead Southern Baptists to be on mission with God."

When the IMB finally reached 5,000 missionaries under appointment in 2001, Southern Baptists considered that a successful fulfillment of "Bold Mission Thrust." But that represented one missionary unit (single adult or family) for every 1.6 million lost people around the world. That's more people than many of our larger cities or smaller states. To expect one, lone missionary unit to evangelize such large population segments is an auspicious challenge. In South Asia there is only one Southern Baptist missionary for every 4.6 million people. There are 140 cities in China alone with more than a million people, and almost half of them do not yet have an evangelical witness. Even before they are all reached, long-range strategies already are focusing on other cities with a population of 250,000 and larger. But if you live in a city smaller than a quarter of a million people, and are in China, there will be no hope of your hearing the gospel in the immediate future and perhaps in your lifetime.

More than 4,000 ethnic, linguistic people groups are identified as unreached, and hundreds of them have no access to the gospel whatsoever. In spite of modern communication and technology which allows us to witness events from all over the world as they occur on our television newscasts, 1.3 billion people have never heard the name of Jesus; they are isolated culturally and geographically from a Christian witness. The task cannot be dependent upon the limited number of missionaries alone. Only as every church and every believer catches a vision for God's purpose and is mobilized to be on mission with God can a lost world be reached and the kingdom of God extended to the ends of the earth.

A Vision Characterized By God's Power

The apostle Paul had a vision and calling that was consistent with God's purpose. God called him to take the gospel to the Gentiles, the non-Jewish peoples and nations of his day. We look to him as a prototype of a cross-cultural missionary. He testified to this calling and mission throughout his epistles and the book of Acts. In Romans 15:18 he described his kingdom vision: "For I will not presume to speak of anything except what Christ has accomplished through me, resulting in the obedience of the Gentiles by word and deed." This may seem to be a parallel to Galatians 2:20 where he said, "I have been crucified with Christ; and it is no longer I who live, but Christ lives in me." It reminds us of the words of Jesus in John 15:5: ". . . apart from Me you can do nothing." But that is not what Paul is saying in Romans 15. It is not simply whatever Christ does through us, but he affirms that the only thing worthy of boasting or speaking about is what we have allowed Christ to do through us to bring the nations to faith, because that is God's purpose.

He goes on to observe in Romans 15:19 that this was done, "in the power of signs and wonders, in the power of the Spirit." It was not what Paul himself had done, but it was the power of God that enabled him to proclaim the gospel and plant churches all the way from Jerusalem to Illyricum. There is only one thing assured of God's power in the Scripture and that is to "be [His] witnesses both in Jerusalem, and in all Judea and Samaria, and even to the remotest part of the earth" (Acts 1:8). We can pray for God's blessing on our church programs, and He will bless them if they are in accord with His will and for His glory, but witnessing to a lost world is the reason He has given us the ·power of the Holy Spirit in our lives.

We must never forget that the Great Commission in Matthew 28:19–20 is preceded by the claim of Christ in verse 18 that, "All authority [power] has been given to Me in heaven and on earth.'" It is because of the power and authority that has been given to Him that we are expected to disciple the nations. He promises to go with us when we go to fulfill His mission. Our vision for the kingdom of God reaching all peoples, even to the most remote part of the earth, is contingent on our efforts being fueled by His power.

For years we prayed for those in communist countries, behind the Iron Curtain, where religious freedom was prohibited and believers were persecuted. In all of our long-range planning and mission strategies, no one imagined the possibility of having missionary personnel witnessing freely in the former Soviet Union or once again serving in

China. Yet today, literally thousands of missionaries and volunteers have swept into those countries. That did not happen as a result of our strategic planning or Western diplomacy, but because of the power and providence of God.

When the walls began to crumble and the doors began to open to the communist world in the early 1990s, we recognized that there was still one formidable barrier to global evangelization remaining, and that was the Muslim world across Northern Africa, the Middle East, and Central Asia. However, following the tragic events of September 11, 2001, personnel throughout these regions began reporting that people there are expressing disillusionment with their Islamic faith. They are questioning a religion that would be used to justify terrorist activity. They are asking questions that reflect a search for hope and security that only Jesus can provide.

Social upheaval, political disruption, economic uncertainty, natural disasters, and wars—so prominent throughout our world today—are being used of God to stir a search for spiritual answers. God said through the prophet Haggai, "I am going to shake the heavens and the earth. I will overthrow the thrones of kingdoms and destroy the power . . . of the nations . . ." (Haggai 2:21–22). It appears this prophecy is being fulfilled as nations are disintegrating and fragmenting due to ethnic conflict, and totalitarian powers are being overthrown. God's power is being manifested that His kingdom might be extended, literally, to the ends of the earth.

Through creative methods, missionaries are able to gain entry and plant their lives in places that would have been unimaginable just a few years ago. Places restricted to a traditional missionary witness are open to Christian teachers, businessmen, social workers, computer consultants, health care personnel, and people serving in a multitude of other professions and roles. There is no limit to what churches and volunteer groups can do when they have a heart for the whole world and will trust the power of God's Spirit to use their presence in a place where people have been deprived of the gospel. In 2002, IMB personnel engaged 146 previously Unreached People Groups with the gospel; the following year 131 more new people groups were touched for the first time. More than half a million baptisms were reported in 2002. That could happen only because of the power of God that indwells the message of the gospel.

A strategy coordinator missionary in China envisioned seeing 200 churches started in his four-year term as he began training national church leaders. But he had to enlarge his vision when more than 200 had been started in six months. Three mosques were closed in a city in Africa because so many of the people became Christian believers. A resistant tribal group in Africa suddenly became responsive and more than 100,000 have been baptized in the last 10 years. In Algeria, seeds of the gospel were planted among Kabyle Berbers and more than 75 churches now line the valley where this group is located. Some researchers report as many as 20,000 new believers coming to faith in Christ every day in China, and Christian believers now number somewhere between 75 million and 100 million in spite of government opposition and restrictions.

Reaching almost 6 billion lost people in our world and more than 4,000 Unreached People Groups exceeds our ability and resources. Devising mission strategies to fulfill the Great Commission is beyond any reasonable and practical means we could possibly imagine. A vision of the kingdoms of this world becoming the kingdom of our Lord can become a reality only when it is characterized by God's power. However, it is not just recognizing God's purpose and understanding the necessity of His power that will lead to personal involvement. We will become obedient to God's mission only when we have a relationship with Him that enables us to identify with His heartbeat and passion for the nations.

A Vision Compelled By God's Passion

We have long made the assumption that if people are made aware of the needs of a lost world, they will respond by giving and praying and maybe even going as a missionary. We don't need a parade of missionaries coming to our churches describing emaciated refugees in Africa or the masses of people in China in bondage to a godless communist dogma in order to understand lostness. We can see it every day on television newscasts and in the headlines of our newspapers. We see live video feeds of Muslim terrorists and suicide bombers as they seek to destroy life. We see the masses of devotees bowing in response to the call to prayer, affirming their allegiance to Allah and Muhammad as his prophet. We witness the despair of victims of earthquakes and natural disasters and the genocide of ethnic conflicts. But we turn off those images in our minds, with no sense of responsibility, as easily as we turn off the television commentator.

We sit comfortably in our pews, pursuing our own plans and aspirations, holding on to the security and comfort of our American lifestyles, never acknowledging that Jesus is the answer to a world in need. He is the Light for a world in spiritual darkness, the hope for multitudes in despair. Even when we realize that we have the answer in our hand and in our hearts, somehow the needs of a lost world do not motivate us to become involved.

I have always assumed that reminding people of the Great Commission would motivate them to at least consider the possibility of going as a missionary. Every Christian and every church should be conscientious about being obedient to what our Lord has commanded us to do. He has clearly told us, "make disciples of all nations . . . to preach the gospel to every creature . . . to be His witnesses . . . to the ends of the earth." However, we apply the Great Commission to whatever we do to witness where we live and choose to label it as "missions." We rationalize away this mandate meant for the church and all of God's people and assume it applies only to an elite few who are called as missionaries. We give token financial support for them to represent us and carry out the Great Commission on our behalf. We assume we are exempt and can pursue our own plans with no responsibility toward those throughout the world who desperately need to hear the good news of Jesus. Southern Baptists have taken pride in now having more than 5,000 international missionaries. But that number represents less than three-tenths of 1 percent of our church membership. Is that all God would call into the fields that are white unto harvest around the world? Does He choose only one out of every 3,000 faithful church members to go and witness to 95 percent of the world's population, while allowing the rest of us to live contentedly among the remaining 5 percent that has abundant opportunity to hear the gospel?

Obviously we are neither motivated by the need nor by the command of our Lord. I came to understand why this might be so in reading a book by J. E. Conant titled *Every Member Evangelism*. In the introduction he comments that the Great Commission is sufficient authority to send us after the lost, but it is not sufficient motivation for us to do so. He goes on to explain that it is not the authority of an external command, even of our Lord, but the impulse of an indwelling presence that will send us after the lost! One would think the mandate and desire of our Lord would motivate us to go. But it is only as we come into a personal relationship with God and we feel His heartbeat for the world that we will be compelled to witness to the lost around us and to go to the ends of the earth. We will have a vision of joining God on mission and being a part of kingdom growth only when we are compelled by God's passion to reach a lost world.

Why did Isaiah sense God's heart for a lost world and respond with a willingness to go? It wasn't a personal call. God did not single out Isaiah, calling him to go to a people in darkness. No, it was a generic call. Isaiah heard God saying, "Whom shall I send and who will go for Us?" (Isaiah 6:8). He didn't wait for God to tap him on the shoulder and say, "You're the one." Isaiah took the initiative and invited God to send him. In essence, he said, "Lord, if you need someone to go to people in darkness, well, here I am. Let me be the one to go."

Why did Isaiah hear God's heart for the people and respond with a submissive spirit? We read in the earlier verses of Isaiah 6 that he had a vision of God high and exalted. He had an experience of coming into His presence, and he recognized God's Lordship and claim on his life. Having entered into that intimate relationship with God, Isaiah felt and shared the passion of God's heart. The motivation for our involvement in God's kingdom plan will not come from denominational programs and church promotion. Putting people on a guilt trip will not produce kingdom growth. It will come only from an intimate relationship with God that results in our being filled with His passion for all peoples.

Occasionally someone asks me, "What is the passion of your life?" I can readily articulate my sense of purpose or what I perceive to be God's will for my life. I can talk about my personal desires, dreams, and visions. But this question always gives me pause. I am passionate about my family, especially my grandchildren. Occasionally I have become quite passionate in rooting for a favorite team at a sporting event. I have been known to express a passion for our missions task. But do these represent the passions of my life? Is there a compelling force, filled with emotion, driving my decisions, focusing my attention, energizing my actions, and motivating my behavior toward a desired accomplishment? Or do I just live life as it comes, accepting whatever may result?

God's passion is for all the peoples of the earth to know and praise Him. He has a passion to be exalted among the nations. Should not God's passion be ours as well? Is there anything other than God's glory among the nations that is worthy of our devotion? His passion for the nations led Him to leave the glories of heaven in order to provide redemption for a lost world. He called Israel to tell of His glory among the nations and has commissioned us to extend His kingdom by making disciples of all nations. We will be motivated to obedience only when we come into such a relationship with God that we know His heart and share His passion.

Several years ago, the International Mission Board began to realize that some significant changes had to be made if we were going to fulfill our vision of "leading Southern Baptists to be on mission with God to bring all the peoples of the world to saving faith in Jesus Christ." The programs and strategies were in place; in fact, we had been doing missions for more than 150 years. It was the purpose for which the Southern Baptist Convention had been formed in 1845. But traditional programs and our historical legacy were not moving us toward vision fulfillment.

1. First of all, we realized we could not be dependent on the limited resources of the IMB but needed to mobilize the resources of Southern Baptists.

Even 5,000 God-called, trained, and equipped missionaries passionately devoted to evangelism could not touch the whole world. We would have to double the number of missionaries just to have one person assigned to each people group. We realized that God had raised up 16 million Southern Baptists, 43,000 churches, 1,200 associations, and 41 state conventions, plus multiple colleges, seminaries, and other entities, all with potential for impacting a lost world. God had blessed and prospered Southern Baptists with numbers and resources, not to take pride in being a great denomination, but to be His people on mission to reach a lost world. When we began to envision the potential of mobilizing and involving our denomination for the purpose to which God had called us as His people, global evangelism became doable.

2. Second, we could no longer take pride in annual statistical growth but we had to measure success and progress only by global impact.

We have always embraced strategic planning. We believed that identifying a clearly defined purpose and objectives and working toward measurable time-defined goals would accomplish more than working randomly, wherever the momentum led. Globally, each region and every local missionary had goals for baptisms, membership growth, and planting churches. Every year we would pat ourselves on the back when the number of baptisms increased, we were able to start a few more churches than the previous year, and we had an increase in the number of missionaries. We were guilty of what Paul described in 2 Corinthians 10:12 as, "measure[ing] themselves by themselves and compare[ing] themselves with themselves."

But we came to the conclusion that significance is not about what we do one year compared to the past year. Success is not determined by how big we are now compared to the past. Certainly we have had success in the past, but seldom would annual statistical reports reflect more than 2- to 3-percent growth. By any standard we were not growing at a rate that would reach a lost world. We realized that the only measure of success is whether or not an impact is being made on a lost world. It is all about lostness and whether or not we are making progress in the gospel becoming accessible to every tribe, language, and nation; that is the vision of God's kingdom.

3. **Finally, we realized our global missions task could not be driven by man-sized goals, but it must be driven by a God-sized vision.**

Seldom would our objectives and strategic planning reflect projections beyond what we realistically felt could be accomplished. There was a tendency to limit our vision by what had been done in the past. We are not capable of reaching the whole world, but if that is God's purpose and plan, then our vision should be no less. We cannot settle for simply extending our witness to a few more countries or engaging an additional number of Unreached People Groups. We could not be satisfied with record numbers of baptisms among established churches where the gospel was already being proclaimed. God's passion and heart is for all peoples. Our vision must be nothing less than seeing all the peoples of the world come to saving faith in Jesus Christ. Our strategies, organization, personnel deployment, and mobilization efforts must be focused and driven by that God-sized vision.

It became evident that implementing these changes in our perspective had to be accompanied by three paradigm shifts:

(1) Personalization instead of generic support.
(2) Partnership instead of exclusive control.
(3) Passion as the motivation instead of program promotion.

Southern Baptists have always been faithful to support their missionaries. They take pride in sending out and supporting more than 5,000 missionaries, but they don't know them, they don't know what they are doing, and they never hear from them. It's no wonder church-based allocations to the Cooperative Program, Southern Baptists' plan for denominational funding, continue to decline. Churches are gravitating more than ever to support para-church and independent mission organizations. Few individuals, relative to our church membership, seem to be open to God's call to overseas work. The International Mission Board is now seeking to discover ways to give churches personalized ownership of the missions task and partnership involvement with missionaries in reaching people groups around the world. But the vision will be driven only by a passion for God's kingdom task of reaching a lost world, not by promotion of the IMB and our denominational programs.

King David had a passion for building the temple, a house of God among His people. In Psalm 132:3–5 he expresses this passion: "Surely I will not enter my house, nor lie on my bed; I will not give sleep to my eyes, or slumber to my eyelids; until I find a place for the Lord, a dwelling place for the Mighty One of Jacob." That must be the passion and vision that motivates us and our churches for kingdom growth. We must not rest, indulge in personal comforts, or be diverted from finding a dwelling place for God among the Tripera, the Tuareg, the Baluchi, the Karalkapak, and all the peoples of the earth.

Occasionally the Global Research Department at the IMB will publish a report on the status of global evangelization. It is a thick computer printout listing line-by-line all the thousands of people groups, many with strange-sounding names, and population segments throughout the world. It identifies those who are being engaged by evangelism strategies, whether or not a missionary is assigned to them, and whether or not other Great Commission groups and organizations may be working with them. It reports if the people group has the Scripture or the *JESUS* film in their own language. It also indicates if a church of local believers has been planted and what percentage of the population currently has access to the gospel.

It is sad to see columns filled with zeroes representing those that still have not been included in anyone's mission strategies and most likely have not yet even heard the name of Jesus. Whenever I see that report on my desk, I don't even have to open it. Knowing the data it contains, the words of John in Revelation 7:9 come to mind. He envisioned the day when Christ would return and see, "a great multitude, which no one could count, from every nation and all tribes and peoples and tongues, standing before the throne and before the Lamb."

That passage puts our mission task in perspective for me. God's mission will be fulfilled. The kingdom of God will grow until it embraces representatives from all nations and peoples—every tribe and language group. The only question is whether or not we will be faithful and obedient to join God in this task to which He calls us as His people.

The Great Commission was not given to the International Mission Board, but to every church, every believer, and every denominational entity. The task of the IMB as a denominational mission entity is not to be the proxy for carrying out Southern Baptist mission efforts, but to channel the support, facilitate the involvement, and to mobilize the resources. Our responsibility and commitment is to enable and empower God's people for kingdom growth to the ends of the earth through a vision that is consistent with God's purpose, a vision that is characterized by God's power, and a vision that is compelled by God's passion.

---

1. Burt Nanus, *Visionary Leadership: Creating a Compelling Sense of Direction for Your Organization* (San Francisco: Jossey-Bass Publishers, July 1995), 3.

Chapter Two

Biblical Foundations for Kingdom Growth

IMB BASIC COMMITMENT:

Obedience to the Lordship of Christ
and God's infallible Word.

IMB BASIC BELIEF:

Jesus Christ is God's only provision for salvation
and people without personal faith in Him are lost
and will spend eternity in hell.

I had no doubt whatsoever regarding my personal call as a missionary as my wife and I were appointed to Indonesia in 1970. I had a strong conviction that the gospel was the power of God to bring all the people of the world to saving faith in Jesus Christ. In fact, I naively envisioned arriving on the shores of one of the largest Muslim countries in the world and watching the pages of Acts unfold once again with multitudes being saved every day! These were people in darkness and spiritual ignorance just waiting for me to arrive. It was amazing to find an open opportunity to witness and share my faith, but I found that people were not especially interested in what I had to share. Oh, there were pockets of responsiveness from a few individuals here and there, but generally their religious convictions, cultural heritage, and social relationships combined to create a resistance to my witness.

In my zeal and enthusiasm I applied myself diligently to learning and applying mission strategies. I busied myself with multiple ministries and efforts to build relationships and establish platforms through which the gospel could be shared. Long days were spent probing village after village, seeking to find a point of contact through which a Bible study, or even an English class, could be started. I became disillusioned when those who expressed an interest in Christ obviously were motivated only by hopes for material gain from this foreigner, help in getting employment, or assistance in obtaining a visa to America.

As the weeks and months progressed with little fruit, my discouragement grew to despondency. Doubts began to plague the confidence I once had in my call and the reliability of God's power. I began to ask myself, "What am I doing here?" Becoming bitter with God, I reasoned that I had been obedient to His call and made the sacrifice to come to Indonesia with my family, but He wasn't keeping His end of the bargain! I was faithfully doing all I knew to do and fully expected Him to produce the hoped-for results.

Motivation began to wane, and one day I found myself lying prostrate on the floor pouring out my heart in dejection, ready to throw in the towel. After a period of complaining and ventilating, God began to quiet my heart and assure me of His presence and sufficiency. I began to recognize and express a yearning to know Him more intimately and to be an instrument worthy to be entrusted with His power.

In that humbling experience of being brought to the end of myself, I was led to recognize the inadequacy of all my efforts, my work, and personal ability. God led me back to the book of Acts. I read His promise in Acts 1:8 that said I would receive power when the Holy Spirit came into my life to be a witness for Christ, and I wondered why there was so little evidence of that power. I came to Acts 4:33 where, "with great power the apostles were giving testimony to the resurrection of the Lord Jesus," and I longed for that power to be evident in my life.

I yearned to see an open door among the people of Indonesia. That desire brought to mind the image expressed in Revelation 3:8 where Jesus said He had set before His witnesses an open door . . . "because you have a little power, and have kept My word, and have not denied My name." And I prayed, "Lord, just a little power; I am not looking for miraculous demonstrations of power, but could I be granted just a little power?"

As I read these passages of Scripture, I began to get a fresh vision of how God worked in the power of the Holy Spirit through the apostles, whom the Bible described as "uneducated and untrained" (Acts 4:13). Then a startling realization hit me. All they did was to lift up Jesus Christ in a bold, positive witness. There was nothing special about them. It was not their abilities or methods, but their faithful witness to the living Christ. It was not what they did but the power of the gospel that drew people to faith in the midst of a hostile environment that was not unlike what I encountered in Indonesia.

I realized that was why God had called me to Indonesia. It was simply to proclaim Christ and lift Him up in a bold, positive witness. I began to get a renewed vision and enthusiasm for my task. I ceased many of the time-consuming programs and ministries in which I had become involved. Instead of creating activities designed to be a platform for witnessing I just began to boldly witness and share Christ. Not everyone responded, but many did.

I was amazed at the spiritual hunger that was reflected in the people who began to be saved. I am still amazed as I think of Muslims in Indonesia coming to faith in Christ. Many of them were rejected by their families. They lost their jobs. They were ostracized by their communities, and a few even had their lives threatened. Why would they turn their backs on their culture, society, and religion to embrace a new religious belief introduced to them by a foreigner? There was really no explanation except the power of God that indwells the message of the gospel.

There were other lessons to be learned in those early years. God had to bring me to the point of futility and failure in order for me to understand my dependence on Him. Upon reflection, I realize a time of renewed commitment was necessary to learn the reliability of God's Word, the reality of His power, and the resources of His grace. Even when all evidence seemed to the contrary, I believed His Word that He loves the whole world, including the people of Indonesia. Jesus died for them, and God's power was sufficient to save them. I saw how the gospel truly was the power of God unto salvation for all who would believe. God had led me to Indonesia, but His call was not so much to a place as it was to be obedient to His Lordship and the teaching of His infallible Word.

That is the basic commitment of the IMB; it is the foundational principle for fulfilling our mission calling. Evangelizing a lost world is not our task or something we as Southern Baptists decided to organize as a convention to do. It is God's mission. And only as we are true to His Word and obedient to His calling do we have the rewarding privilege of joining Him to extend His kingdom to the ends of the earth. We cannot presume to simply devise mission strategies and implement programs for reaching a lost world. All we do must be guided by God's Word and predicated on submission to the dynamic leadership of our living Lord who is seeking to be known among all peoples.

Obedience To A Biblical Worldview

Obedience to the Lordship of Jesus Christ and to the Bible as our sole authority of faith and practice are the foundational principles for our mission task as well as our Baptist beliefs. Plans and programs can be quite diverse. Goals and directions can take one in any direction. We are engaged in many worthy strategies and ministries that will result in evangelizing and discipling the nations and peoples of the world. But all we do must be superseded by a higher commitment to Jesus Christ—the eternal, incarnate, living Son of God.

He Himself claimed in Matthew 28:18 that all power and authority had been given to Him. He then called us to obedience in discipling the nations. Commitment is the deliberate, volitional yielding of oneself to a principle or cause. Obedience is subjection of oneself to a specific authority that supersedes an independent course of action. Jesus is our Savior and Lord; obedience to His commands and commitment to follow His revealed will are not optional.

Although the IMB, as a mission agency, is accountable to the churches of our denomination, all we do must be consistent with the leadership of Jesus Christ and His Word. Obedience to His Lordship demands that churches and believers, as well, keep all other levels of authority and administrative decision-making in subjection to His calling and purpose, and that we do everything for His glory.

While prayer is the channel of communication with the Father through which we discern His will in specific situations, the Bible is an absolutely reliable and trustworthy revelation of God's truth. It is wholly inspired by God and is eternally relevant for all matters of faith and practice, including our mission methods in reaching a lost world. The Bible clearly defines our mission to proclaim the gospel to all people without exception, to baptize converts, disciple believers, equip the saints, and extend the kingdom of God through the multiplication of congregations or churches in the pattern of the New Testament.

Our responsibility is not just to proclaim the gospel as Scripture commands, but to conform our methodology to biblical models and teaching. We must not neglect ministering to the suffering, feeding the hungry, and liberating the oppressed, as our Savior demonstrated in compassionate actions and teaching. We must remain doctrinally sound in discipling believers and training leaders so that churches resulting from our efforts propagate solid Baptist beliefs. If we are to be effective, we must reflect the pattern of relationships and mutual submission to one another that is the product of a servant spirit. The ultimate purpose of this is that all things would be to the praise of God the Father and our obedience would result in His being made known and exalted among all peoples.

Missionaries are often criticized for seeking to "proselytize" other faiths and are accused of disrupting indigenous cultures. Neither charge is valid. It does no good whatsoever just to change from one religion to another, whether as the result of coercion, incentives, or a personal decision of conscience, for just following a religion is a futile effort of man to connect with God. The only thing that matters is a personal relationship with God that comes through believing in Jesus Christ. This is because only Christ, through His death on the cross and resurrection, has removed the barrier of sin, enabling one to be reconciled with a holy and righteous God.

As we become more aware of Unreached People Groups who have never heard of Jesus, we tend to rationalize their spiritual condition. They are isolated culturally and geographically where there is no church. They have their religious rituals, their gods, and their cultural traditions. It is often thought that a loving and merciful God would not send them to hell should they die without ever hearing of Jesus. Many tend to think that because of their ignorance and sincerity, there must be another way for them to be saved.

That conclusion would be partially correct, for God does not condemn them to hell; they are condemned by their sin. The Bible says in Romans 3:23, "all have sinned and fall short of the glory of God," and in Romans 6:23, "the wages of sin is death." All who have never come to repentance and faith in Jesus Christ are condemned by their own sin. It is sin that separates them from a holy and righteous God. The idea of a "noble savage" with a pure and sincere heart serving the gods of his culture is a myth. People everywhere are sinners with a depraved nature, just like us.

The apostle Paul said of his own Jewish brethren in Romans 10:1–2, "Brethren, my heart's desire and my prayer to God for them is for their salvation. For I testify about them that they have a zeal for God, but not in accordance with knowledge." He had said in Romans 9:3 that he himself would be willing to be condemned if they could be saved. These were people who worshiped the true and living God and sought to follow His laws, but they were lost. How much more are those who have no knowledge of the truth? The reality of universal sin provides no other alternative for people to be saved except by faith in Jesus Christ.

Let's suppose for a moment that there was some possibility, due to the mercies of God, that those peoples who have never heard the gospel could be saved. They live a lifetime and die never knowing of Jesus. They cannot be held accountable for rejecting Christ, so perhaps God would make some kind of provision by which they will be saved. If that were true, our most effective mission strategy would be silence. We should determine never to speak the name of Jesus again lest someone who has never heard should hear and subsequently be accountable for his sin.

But that is not what the Bible tells us. The pages of God's Word are filled with the urgent command to make disciples of all nations, to preach the gospel to every creature, to be witnesses to the ends of the earth. The promise of a Redeemer was given that all the earth might look to Him and be saved. Israel, as God's people, was called to tell of His salvation and declare His glory that God would be exalted among all people. God would not have gone to the extent of sacrificing His Son had there been any other way for people to be saved. Jesus said in John 14:6, "I am the way, and the truth, and the life; no one comes to the Father, but through me." The disciples declared in Acts 4:12, "There is salvation in no one else; for there is no other name under heaven that has been given among men, by which we must be saved."

We don't have the option of viewing a lost world from any perspective other than that described in God's Word. The Bible reveals Jesus as the only way and hope of salvation. Those who have never come to Him in repentance and faith are lost, whether they have rejected the gospel or never heard. For those who claim to know Christ and to be His followers, obedience to what He has told us to do is not optional. We, as His people, are to be His witnesses to the ends of the earth. We have a responsibility to proclaim the gospel that all peoples would have the opportunity to hear and respond to God's love and embrace the kingdom of God.

Our society has become pluralistic. Postmodern influences have convinced many—including some in our churches—that there is no absolute truth or singular way to God. We have befriended Hindu neighbors. We encounter Muslims in shopping malls and Buddhists in the restaurants of our community. They all appear to be good citizens, have fine families, and are considerate of others. Surely, we reason, they are just as saved in the religion they choose to follow as Christians are. We are accused of being narrow-minded, intolerant, and arrogant for sending missionaries to other religions and cultures and attempting to convert them to our way of life. There is much to commend in other religions. They provide many common elements of ethical teaching and social responsibility, yet none can offer assurance of salvation from sin.

There is much we believe in our Christian theology regarding God and man, but conviction regarding the uniqueness of Christ is basic in compelling us to fulfill our mission of proclaiming Him to all the world. He is the only way of salvation from sin and for anyone to be reconciled with a holy and righteous God. This is truly good news for a lost world. It is a conviction and belief that must be proclaimed. It is a message that all peoples deserve to hear, and our Lord has instructed us to bear witness of this truth everywhere.

It would not have been necessary in previous generations to state our obvious belief that Jesus Christ is God's only provision for salvation and that people without personal faith in Him are lost and will spend eternity in hell. Not too many years ago that reality was just assumed. But our conviction concerning a world without Christ and the consequences of sin has been eroded. Yet hell is real, and eternity is long. The soul of man does not cease to exist at physical death, nor is there a spiritual annihilation for those who do not know God. Hell is a destiny of everlasting torment that is irreversible once one passes from this earthly life. It does not matter whether one has heard and rejected the gospel or never had an opportunity to hear and know God's provision for salvation. Obviously, there would be no basis for doing missions were this not true.

God, in His love and mercy, has made provision for the world to be saved. Romans 10:13 says, "Whoever will call on the name of the Lord will be saved." But then we are confronted with the question in the following verses, "How then will they call on Him in whom they have not believed? How will they believe in Him whom they have not heard? And how will they hear without a preacher? How will they preach unless they are sent?" The mandate is compelling. We are to go and proclaim Jesus as the way and the only hope of salvation from sin. Our sharing the gospel is not optional. Restricting the geographical scope of our witness to where we live is not optional. Neither has the church been given the option whether or not to send and support missionaries and to be a part of kingdom growth to the ends of the earth.

THE IMPERATIVE OF IMPACTING LOSTNESS

Missions is all about lostness and glorifying God by extending His kingdom until He is known and exalted by all the peoples of the earth. It is not simply a matter of statistical growth—tallying the number of missionaries sent out or proclaiming the gospel wherever we can for whatever may result. It is not about doing humanitarian work, though that is a part of our responsibility as believers and often a channel of effective witness. It is not about planting a church here and there, providing people a place of worship, or an evangelism blitz for a week or two and then going home. Missions is making the gospel accessible to all the peoples of the world so that those in darkness can come to the Light of the world. Evangelism is proclaiming a message of hope for those in despair and salvation for a world in sin. Kingdom growth is extending the witness of God's kingdom to touch every language and culture.

Significant progress in taking the gospel to all peoples has been made in recent years. In 1995 the AD2000 and Beyond organization sponsored a Global Consultation on World Evangelization in Seoul, South Korea. More than 4,000 people from 180 countries gathered for the explicit purpose of conferring on how the Great Commission could be completed by the year 2000 in terms of planting a church within every people group in the world. It was an auspicious goal that was obviously not met, but it did accelerate global mission efforts. At that time researchers reported 2,161 ethnic-linguistic people groups that had not been touched by the gospel. Many of them had a population numbering in the millions. These people groups represented a cumulative population of 1.68 billion people who had not yet even heard the name of Jesus.

By 2004 that number of people groups had dropped to fewer than three hundred, mostly smaller micropeople groups. Mission agencies have adjusted priorities and refocused resources to reach all peoples. However, there still remain almost 6,525 people groups—as many as 3.4 billion people—who are less than 2 percent evangelized and are identified as "unreached." Although there are some churches within their countries, and Christian materials are available in their language, most of the people do not have access to a Christian witness.

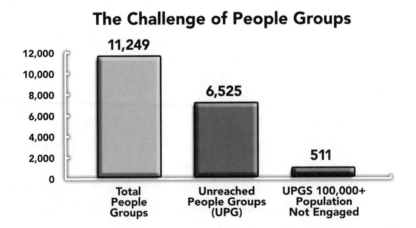

The Challenge of People Groups

Elsewhere, there are countries where missionaries have been able to proclaim the gospel. There is Christian media and literature, Bibles are readily available, and churches have grown to reach up to

10 percent or more of the population. However, 2 billion people in these countries are adherents of other religions and have not in any form or fashion declared their faith in Jesus Christ.

Status of Global Evangelization Model

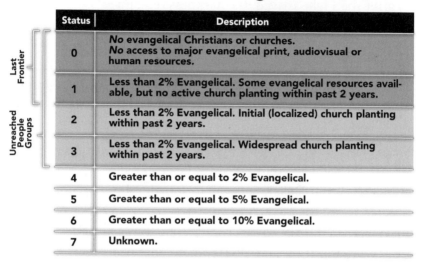

	Status	Description
Last Frontier	0	*No evangelical Christians or churches. No access to major evangelical print, audiovisual or human resources.*
	1	Less than 2% Evangelical. Some evangelical resources available, but no active church planting within past 2 years.
Unreached People Groups	2	Less than 2% Evangelical. Initial (localized) church planting within past 2 years.
	3	Less than 2% Evangelical. Widespread church planting within past 2 years.
	4	Greater than or equal to 2% Evangelical.
	5	Greater than or equal to 5% Evangelical.
	6	Greater than or equal to 10% Evangelical.
	7	Unknown.

Jesus made the contrast clear. There is no equivocation in distinguishing the truth found in Him alone from that claimed by all other religious and cultural traditions. He could not have affirmed it more strongly as His argument with the Pharisees reached a peak of confrontation. "Then Jesus again spoke to them, saying, 'I am the Light of the world; he who follows Me will not walk in the darkness, but will have the Light of life'" (John 8:12). Those who have come to faith in Jesus are in the light of God's truth. They have become a part of His eternal kingdom; whereas those who do not believe in Jesus as Savior and Lord are in darkness. He continued that analogy and put the global, eternal purpose of His mission to redeem a lost world into perspective when He quoted the prophet Isaiah. In Matthew 4:16 He said, "'The people who were sitting in darkness saw a great light, and to those who were sitting in the land and shadow of death, upon them a light dawned.'"

That Light began its unquenchable illumination as the dawning of the resurrection morning overpowered the darkness that had enveloped the cross. Generations of missionaries and Christian witnesses have continued to proclaim the Light to those who are lost and literally dwell under the shadow of death in spiritual darkness. Yet 2,000 years after the Light arrived, the darkness remains.

Across a relatively evangelized African continent, pockets of darkness remain where fetishes and witch doctors hold people in bondage to ancient fears and superstitions. Faster than a Christian witness can be shared, the haunting specter of AIDS claims more than 6,000 lives a day, decimating the wage-earners of society and leaving millions of orphans. When David Livingstone arrived in Africa more than a century ago he spoke of seeing the smoke of a thousand villages. Many of those villages still have yet to receive the gospel.

On a trip from Dakar, Senegal, to Johannesburg in South Africa, I expected to see the poverty of crowded, inner-city ghettos and destitute villages in the dry, barren countryside. I was surprised to see the degree of urbanization and development that had occurred in many areas of Africa. Yet the social deterioration, political instability, and ethnic warfare that are rampant have left the quality of life in shambles. Crime, illiteracy, and joblessness leave a pall of hopelessness over the people. Sadder still is the hopelessness beyond this life for masses. There are 1,521 Unreached People Groups south of the Sahara who do not know Jesus.

I'll never forget my first trip to Russia soon after the fall of communism. Our group felt an element of disbelief as we walked through Red Square, saw the grandeur of historical landmarks, and attended the ballet *Swan Lake* in Moscow's Hall of Congress. But what I remember most is the lingering impression of oppressiveness, the sullen demeanor of the people, and the drabness of our surroundings. I remember our missionaries living in small, cramped apartments, trying to relate to suspicious neighbors, coping with limited consumer goods, and tolerating long, cold winters in order to share the Light of the world with those so long deprived of religious freedom.

A subsequent trip to India reinforced the intensity of how dark the world can be without Christ. I had arrived in Delhi during the Kumbh Mela festival—the largest religious gathering in the world. Once every three years this three-month event is held at one of the four holy cities on the Ganges River. That year the festival was in Hardiwar, where more than 10 million Hindu devotees gathered to bathe in the waters of the river, believing that act would wash away all sin. As we stood on the rooftop of a nearby building gazing on the panorama before us, my heart was broken. As we watched the massive congestion of humanity scurrying about to get into the frigid waters flowing down from the Himalayas, I felt I was looking down on an anthill that someone had stepped on! But that was only a precursor to the experience a couple of days later while visiting the Kali temple in Calcutta.

In the midst of pungent incense and clanging bells, pilgrims crowded into the temple courtyard. The altar before the black, blood-thirsty, multiheaded goddess of Calcutta flowed with blood as people brought goats and sacrificed them. Devotees rushed forward, dipping their fingers in the blood and pressing it to their foreheads. They did not know that it is not the blood of calves and goats, but the precious blood of our Lord Jesus Christ that cleanses from sin. Idol worship is not just an ancient phenomenon depicted among uneducated and unenlightened pagan tribes in biblical days. It is a reality throughout the world today.

Some researchers consider places such as Latin America or Western Europe to be evangelized. Although steeples of churches and cathedrals punctuate the skyline of every city and village, the lostness is overwhelming. Some of the greatest barriers to people knowing Jesus are not in the Hindu or Muslim world—among animists and unreached peoples—but in places where people think they are Christians. Never mind that they have never read the Bible and attend church only for weddings and funerals, their self-identity is "Christian." They have a false security that creates a smug satisfaction that is difficult to penetrate with the claims of Christ.

In some ways it is difficult to discern the difference in cultural Catholics of South America—with their penance before icons, trust in charms, and ritualistic prayers—from a similar pattern of Hindu worship in India. Though churches abound throughout Latin America, spiritism has perverted Catholic doctrine in a syncretism that claims more adherents than evangelical believers. To travel through Mexico City with 21.2 million people, and São Paulo, Brazil, with 19 million, and the other urban areas of the continent overwhelms me with the massive challenge of lostness.

But the most foreboding and formidable barrier to kingdom growth remains in the Muslim world across Northern Africa, the Middle East, and into Central Asia. Response to the gospel is accelerating in Africa and Latin America. The frontiers of Asia are seeing an increasing harvest as a Christian witness sweeps across previously untouched frontiers. But for centuries the followers of Islam have strengthened their stranglehold on the Arab world and neighboring countries. Restrictive policies have kept any Christian presence to a minimum and prohibited open witness. The shrill sound of the minarets, calling the people to prayer five times a day, bears testimony of the lostness of multitudes with little chance of hearing of a God who loves them and offers grace for salvation. They have a firmly ingrained belief in a fatalistic religion controlled by a punitive god who cannot be known.

On a recent trip to the region, I stood on a hillside above the city of Damascus in Syria at dusk. It was time for Magrib, the evening prayer. We heard the first faint sound of the call to prayer from a distant mosque. Others rapidly followed as a growing crescendo of loud speakers calling the faithful to prayer swept across this city of 2.4 million people. As each local mosque joined the cacophony of sound, green lights came on, illuminating the hundreds of minarets spread across the valley below us. We were told that there are only a handful of evangelical believers in all of Syria. My heart cried, "How long, Lord, before these people for whom You died have the privilege of knowing You?" I prayed that He would reveal Himself as He did to Paul on the road to this city years ago, when an adversary of Christ was changed to become an ambassador of the gospel. When will these people, still in an adversarial relationship to Christ, be changed by embracing the gospel?

I had a similar experience in Central Asia just a few months earlier. I had just completed a tour of some of the "Stans"—Kazakhstan, Kyrgyzstan, Tajikistan, Uzbekistan, and Azerbaijan—newly independent republics that broke off from the Soviet Union. Centuries of Islamic indoctrination had been brushed with a veneer of atheism from 70 years of communist domination. As we traveled through country after country, I was thrilled to see evidence of the gospel being sown. Missionary personnel told of widespread spiritual hunger. They gave exciting reports of new churches being planted and discipling and training national believers.

It was the final night of the journey. We were enjoying dinner with our regional leadership team in a mountainside restaurant overlooking the city of Almaty. Behind us were the snow-capped Tanshin Mountains separating Kazakhstan from China. We discussed the 12 million unreached Uighur people who straddled that border. Information about this Unreached People Group stimulated a question I had not thought to ask as we rejoiced in all the peoples who were hearing the gospel. I asked how many people groups in these Central Asian republics have been engaged with the gospel and churches planted among them. The reply was 60!

This led to an obvious subsequent question. I asked, "How many people groups have not yet been reached in the region?" The response was so shocking it caused an immediate pause in conversation. The regional leader responded with deep emotion that there were 300 people groups still waiting for someone to tell them of Christ. "The most difficult thing about being regional leader for Central Asia," he continued, "is having to decide in our strategic planning, with such limited resources and personnel, which people groups will be deprived of the gospel yet another year." I boarded the plane and flew home the next day with the question burning in my heart, "By what criteria should any people be deprived of hearing the gospel?"

I believe we will be held accountable by God for every person who dies in sin and goes to hell without ever having an opportunity to hear, understand, and respond to the gospel. His desire is for none to perish but for all to come to repentance (2 Peter 3:9). He has committed to us as His followers the task of proclaiming the good news. But also, if there will be a judgment of God upon His people for lack of obedience, it will be for our failure to reap the harvest where people are open and responsive. But we are not just to witness where we live or where people are responsive. We are to take the gospel to everyone so that God's kingdom can be extended to the ends of the earth.

God has opened doors of opportunity that we would never have imagined just a few years ago. There are people living in darkness, desperate for a message of hope, still waiting for someone to come and tell them. God has blessed us so richly. The gospel has become so familiar and commonplace that we take it for granted. In our prayer meetings we pray for Aunt Sally, who is sick, to be healed and that others in the hospital would recover and not die. Most of our prayers are focused on the sick and infirm, extending their lives and keeping them out of heaven for the time being. But do we utter a prayer to get the peoples of the world into heaven?

When will we take seriously our obedience to what our Lord Jesus Christ has told us to do about reaching the nations? How will we give account to our Lord for our neglect as we lay before Him our beautiful, well-appointed buildings? As we tell Him of all our church programs that blessed and served the community of the redeemed, how will we justify the little that was given and few who went to bring the nations and peoples of the world into His kingdom? It has been said by many, "Why should anyone hear the gospel twice before everyone has had a chance to hear it once?"

The apostle Paul uses an interesting term for the gospel with reference to those who have never heard it. He calls it the "mystery" of God. Ephesians 1:9 reads, "He made known to us the **mystery** of His will," and goes on to describe God's eternal plan before the foundation of the world of redemption through Jesus Christ. In chapter 3, verses 3 through 5, Paul shares his testimony and says, "that by revelation there was made known to me the **mystery** . . . which in other generations was not known to the sons of men, as it has now been revealed to His holy apostles and prophets in the Spirit." By referring to the gospel as a mystery, he doesn't mean that it is something spooky or mysterious. The word translated "mystery" in the New Testament is the word, *musterion.* It literally means that which is covered or unknown. It is unrevealed, and therefore is a mystery. God had given the prophets a glimpse of this mystery, but only recently did the apostles, including Paul, come to understand it as the Holy Spirit revealed it to them. But to past generations it was a mystery.

One of the most grievous passages in the Bible reveals the tragedy of the gospel remaining a mystery. First Corinthians 2:7–8 states, "but we speak God's wisdom in a **mystery**, the hidden wisdom, which God predestined before the ages to our glory; the wisdom which none of the rulers of this age has understood; for if they had understood it, they would not have crucified the Lord of glory." The rulers rejected Christ because they did not know or understand the mystery of God's wisdom!

There are many who have heard and rejected the gospel, but the tragedy in our world today is that most of the people of the world are bound for hell because they have not heard the good news of Christ. It remains a mystery to them. They do not know that God sent His only Son to die on the cross and that He was raised again to give them victory over sin and death. Multitudes who long for hope and assurance continue in darkness and despair because no one has revealed that mystery to them.

Paul requested prayer in Ephesians 6:19 that "utterance may be given to me in the opening of my mouth, to make known with boldness the **mystery** of the gospel." We are told in 1 Corinthians 4:1–2 that as servants of Christ we are "stewards of the **mysteries** of God . . . moreover, it is required of stewards that one be found trustworthy." Those of us who have received the gospel—to whom the mystery has been revealed—have a stewardship to share that message with others and to make it known.

The countries we visited on that trip to Central Asia—where missionaries have only recently gained entry—were the places visited by the renowned Marco Polo several centuries ago. He and his father set out from Venice in 1271, destined for the courts of Kublai Khan, grandson of the infamous Genghis Khan, who ruled the massive Mongol empire of what is now China and beyond. It was 24 years before Marco Polo returned home. The silk, spices, and jewels he displayed tantalized Europeans and opened a virtual highway of commerce across the trade routes of Central Asia. The routes multiplied as the caravans of ancient days responded to these new markets. For 800 years the braided trails leading East have been called the Silk Road.

That identity certainly described the product rather than the smoothness and convenience of those treks across expansive deserts and treacherous mountain passes. Crossing the Bosporus Straits at Istanbul, traders passed through Tabriz in northwestern Iran, continued across Persia into what is now Afghanistan, through northern Pakistan and over the Himalayas into Kashgar in northwestern China. Later caravans established more lucrative northern routes through Bukhara and Samarkand, now in Uzbekistan, where massive mosques and blue-domed tombs attest to the affluence such trade brought to these ancient empires. They touched what have become the modern-day capital cities of Baku, Tashkent, Bishkek, and Dushanbe. The development of these trade routes and how they brought together Oriental and European civilizations is an intriguing history. But the tragic side of the countries and peoples that span the ancient Silk Road is their lostness.

Marco Polo's father and uncle had been to China before. Impressed with the teachings of Christian civilization, Kublai Khan had asked the Polos to bring a hundred Christian teachers to introduce his empire to these beliefs from the West. That request and open door of opportunity was never fulfilled. They were able to enlist only two friars, who turned back early in the subsequent journey. Kublai Khan and his empire embraced the teachings of Buddhist monks from India and Burma. Lands that lay along the western end of the road adopted the religion of Arab merchants, and these trade routes became the means for spreading the Islamic faith instead of the Christian message.

Today the peoples along that ancient Silk Road pose a formidable challenge to kingdom growth. But God is opening the doors to believers willing to plant their lives among them. He is providing channels of access among those so long deprived of the gospel. And He also is opening the hearts of people who are searching for a hope and security that cannot be found in their traditions. Global events are now focusing our attention on this area of the world. Could it be that the request of Kublai Khan 800 years ago might finally be granted? Could God be shaking the Muslim world through tragic events motivated by terrorist hatred to break down the last massive stronghold of religious resistance to the gospel?

Spices, jewels, and modern-day commercial products still flow across the mountains and valleys of the Silk Road through Turkey, Iraq, Iran, Afghanistan, Pakistan, and Central Asia. Will we join God in this unprecedented opportunity to carry that which has never before penetrated these trade routes, the gospel of Jesus Christ? This area may literally be the ends of the earth to which Christ expects us to be witnesses. The Bible is clear. Our responsibility is to all peoples. God is moving in power and providence to extend His kingdom. Will we be obedient?

During my first trip to Central Asia about 10 years earlier, I had gathered one night for fellowship with pioneer missionaries who had ventured into this region. They had boldly seized the opportunity to fill new and challenging assignments. As we prayed, one of them voiced a prayer that disrupted my meditation. He voiced praise to God for the 70 years the Soviet Union had dominated the peoples of Central Asia. I thought it strange he would be thankful for that communist regime, knowing its atheistic ideology that dominated the people and prohibited religious freedom. Later I asked him why he prayed as he did. In reply he explained that for centuries the great universities and mosques of Central Asia had been strategic in propagating Islam across their trade routes and among the populous cities. "But," he said, "in a mere 70 years the atheistic influence of the Soviet Union has emasculated this Muslim stronghold, leaving the people empty, spiritually destitute, and responsive to the gospel in this time of harvest."

What we see happening in the world today is really not a result of IMB strategies and Western diplomacy. It is the power of God shaking nations and societies that His kingdom might extend to the ends of the earth. God's providence is behind world events; He has not relinquished His sovereignty over the nations. And when we read of political disruptions, social upheaval, economic deterioration, wars, and natural disasters, He is creating an environment where people cannot look to their culture, traditions, and religion but only to our Lord Jesus Christ for salvation and hope. Like Esther, He has called us into the kingdom for such a time as this!

How can the darkness be dispelled so that those who dwell in darkness may have the Light of life? The answer is found in a hymn not often sung these days, but it expresses the biblical foundations for kingdom growth—"We've a Story to Tell." That's it! All we have and really need is a simple story, the story of the gospel. It is truly a story of truth and mercy, a story of peace and light. Within the message of that story is the power to dispel the darkness. Romans 1:16 says, "The gospel . . . is the power of God for salvation to everyone who believes, to the Jew first and also to the Greek." Because the story is being told and many are hearing the gospel for the first time, the chorus of that hymn is becoming a reality.

> For the darkness shall turn to dawning,
> And the dawning to noonday bright,
> And Christ's great kingdom shall come on earth,
> The kingdom of love and light.

This is the reason God allowed the light to shine in our hearts and for us to know the mystery of the gospel; it is so that we will pray, we will give, and we will go to a world that is still in darkness. Second Corinthians 4:6 tells us, "For God, who said, 'Light shall shine out of darkness,' is the One who has shone in our hearts to give the Light of the knowledge of the glory of God in the face of Christ." Can you imagine the excitement and anticipation of our Heavenly Father when we came to the Light and embraced Jesus Christ as our Savior? He saw the potential of another witness who would faithfully proclaim the Light of the world to the peoples still in darkness. It expanded His hope of the kingdom being extended to the ends of the earth.

The prophet Isaiah reminds us of the darkness that covers the earth but assures us that the power of light will dispel the darkness. "Arise, shine; for your light has come, and the glory of the Lord has risen upon you. For behold, darkness will cover the earth, and deep darkness the peoples; but the Lord will rise upon you . . . and nations will come to your light . . ." (Isaiah 60:1–3). Just as turning on a light switch in a darkened room dispels the darkness, so will our witness dispel the darkness among the nations. The light doesn't have to struggle to overcome the dark, for it is the very nature of the light to prevail. But until we are willing to go, in obedience to our Lord and our biblical mission to share the light, the peoples will remain in darkness.

I cannot wipe from my mind an illustration I once read. It is quite familiar and has been used in pulpits for a long time to encourage more conscientious involvement in evangelism. The picture is that final judgment day when we will don our white robes of righteousness and be welcomed into the eternal glory of heaven. It will be a time of celebration and rejoicing as we give glory to the Lamb of God who redeemed us from sin. But across a great chasm will be a multitude of people with bowed heads and sad countenances entering an eternity of torment in hell. These are those who never heard or responded to the message of salvation. They will look at us with forlorn reconciliation to their fate, and that look will say, "You knew! But you never came and told us; we never had an opportunity to know."

But sadder still will be the eyes of our Lord. In one of those paradoxes of the Christian faith, even as He receives us with joy, His heart will be broken over the multitudes who never knew He died for them. I believe His eyes will meet ours much as they did Peter's on that night of denial, and without a word will communicate, "I told you to go. I promised you My power. I assured you of My grace, but you chose to stay at home, to hold on to your comfort and security and were unwilling to go that My kingdom could be extended to the ends of the earth."

We have been called to obedience. No one is exempt from the teaching and mandate of Scripture that reveals the heart of God for a lost world. A commitment to the Lordship of Jesus Christ means a commitment to carrying out His will and proclaiming the gospel to a lost world. Scripture does not limit our realm of responsibility to where we live, but as the people of God we are the ones to carry the gospel to the ends of the earth. It is about lostness. And if we don't take the gospel to the lost—wherever they are—who will? We believe in an inerrant and infallible Word of God; may we also be fully committed to living out the Word and being obedient to what it teaches us to do.

CHAPTER THREE

EMPOWERING KINGDOM GROWTH
THROUGH PRAYER

IMB CORE VALUE:

Our basic means of understanding and
fulfilling God's mission is prayer.

Early in my tenure as president of the International Mission Board, I spoke at a missions week at Ridgecrest Baptist Assembly in North Carolina. In my message I mentioned that the board had recently appointed our first missionary unit to serve openly in Albania. Previously field staff had been engaged in a strategic consortium with other Great Commission Christians to reach the Albanian people, but this was the first missionary visa to be granted to one of our personnel.

After the service a lady approached me. She was crying and obviously overcome with emotion. She asked, "Do we really have a missionary in Albania?" I assured her that we did. After a moment she gained her composure and explained that seven years earlier she had read that Albania was the most atheistic country in the world, prohibiting worship and restricting any kind of religious expression. She had called the Foreign Mission Board, as we were known then, to ask what we were doing in Albania. She was told that the country was closed to a missionary presence, and there was nothing we could do but pray.

"I went back to my church and asked our ladies' group to pray for Albania," she said. "For seven years we have been praying for Albania!" When I heard that, I began to weep with her. There is no doubt in my mind that the doors to Albania opened to the gospel because a group of ladies in a small Southern Baptist church had a heart for a lost nation and interceded in prayer before the throne of God.

Certainly there were circumstances that brought about the change, such as the collapse of communism in Eastern Europe. But those who have seen global changes open doors long closed to the gospel readily acknowledge that God, in His sovereign power over nations, moves in response to the prayers of His people. Strongholds crumble and response to the gospel accelerates when we pray.

God gives us an amazing promise in Psalm 2:8. He says, "Ask of me and I will surely give the nations as Your inheritance, and the very ends of the earth as Your possession." But how often do we pray for the Sudan, Libya, Afghanistan, and countries such as Eritrea, Bhutan, and Chad? Do we fervently plead for Unreached People Groups like the Drukpa, the Mazaderani, the Acehnese, and Baluchi? Is it any wonder that generation after generation continues in the bondage of darkness and sin while God yearns to draw them into His kingdom?

God's desire is to be exalted among the nations. Christ died for the whole world. We are told in Psalm 22:27–28 that one day, "All the ends of the earth will remember and turn to the Lord, and all the families of the nations will worship before You. For the kingdom is the Lord's, and He rules over the nations." But how long will it be until all the nations have an opportunity to hear and respond to the gospel? How long will it be until they are set free from the powers of darkness and acknowledge Jesus Christ as King of kings and Lord of lords?

Isn't Satan clever! He gets us to limit our praying to personal matters—our personal needs and concerns, our families, our communities, and our churches—and it never occurs to us to intercede for the nations. His strongholds remain secure against the kingdom of God when we never pray for the nations and intercede for the peoples of the world. Prayer is not peripheral to missions strategy. It is not to undergird and support mission strategy. It is the *heart* of our strategy to reach the nations and fulfill the Great Commission. Someone has said that the battle for the nations will be won on the knees of God's people. Missionaries are sent in for the mopping up exercises!

Missionaries labor faithfully and struggle in resistant fields, but the harvest never seems to come because God's people are not praying. Missionaries fight discouragement and persevere in the face of religious opposition, government restrictions, illness, and conflict. Churches and faithful supporters voice their "GBM prayers" (God bless the missionaries) but with a shallow concern that doesn't bother to lift specific needs and plead for the people those missionaries are seeking to reach.

Charles Haddon Spurgeon linked the action of God with the prayers of His people. He said, "God will bless Elijah and send rain on Israel, but Elijah must pray for it. If the chosen nation is to prosper, Samuel must plead for it. If the Jews are to be delivered, Daniel must intercede. God will bless Paul, and the nations will be converted, but Paul must pray ... Let me have your prayers, and I can do anything! Let me be without my people's prayers, and I can do nothing."[1]

Why would God, who is sovereign over the nations, limit what He does to the prayers of His people? This is a God who said in Isaiah 14:24, "Surely, just as I have intended so it has happened, and just as I have planned so it will stand." In Isaiah 46:9–10 He says, "Remember the former things long past, for I am God, and there is no other; I am God, and there is no one like Me, declaring the end from the beginning and from ancient times things which have not been done, saying, 'My purpose will be established, and I will accomplish all My good pleasure.'" The Scripture reveals a God who reigns over the earth and in His providence is moving through all things to accomplish His predetermined will.

The word "providence" comes from two Latin words: *video* which means "to see," and *pro* which, when added as a prefix, means "to see beforehand." God is able to see beforehand history and all that is going to transpire—He knows the end from the beginning—and plans to use it to accomplish His purpose. He calls us to prayer that we might know His heart and have the privilege of getting in on what He is doing. Proverbs 16:9 reminds us that "The mind of man plans His way, but the Lord directs his steps."

So why does He call us to pray for the nations? Because when we intercede for the nations and pray for the peoples God is seeking to draw into His kingdom, we share His heart and join Him in reaching them. As we communicate with the Father, we begin to share His burden and become responsive to what God wants us to do.

Does God know how the peoples of the world are to be reached? Of course! Does He know which churches and people will be called out to be His instruments to reach each specific people group? Yes. He knows which ones will respond as the result of a testimony of a missionary, a mission trip, or just a news event. He knows those who, with an obedient heart, will begin to pray. And once those prayers begin, God is able to move in human hearts and direct His people to implement His plan.

Sometime ago I heard Henry Blackaby speak to a group of missionaries. They were strategy coordinators, the team leaders responsible for designing strategies to impact Unreached People Groups and for coordinating the efforts of their coworkers. Each one had a passion for his adopted people. Blackaby asked each one if he believed God wanted his people group to come to saving faith in Jesus Christ. He asked them if they believed God desired a church-planting movement to make the gospel accessible to all the people.

To each question everyone responded with unequivocal affirmation. Then Blackaby followed up with a sequential question, saying, "Now, God wants to reach your people, but He doesn't have a clue how that can be done, so He has called you to figure it out and try to develop a strategy. Is that what He expects you to do?" Of course this was just a rhetorical question, and he proceeded to explain that, in

God's providence and sovereignty over the nations, He already knows how and when they are going to be reached. His point to this group of strategy coordinators was for them to give priority to knowing God and discerning where and how God is working, and then join Him in what He is doing.

THE MEANS FOR DISCERNING GOD'S WILL

Prayer is the means by which we discern God's will. It is the channel of communication by which God can reveal Himself and stir our hearts to join Him where He is working. Without prayer, as an individual or a church, we are left to our own devices, wisdom, and insight, and the result is usually a struggle to make things happen, to make our programs successful. Prayer opens our hearts to hear God calling us as we pray for Him to call out laborers into the harvest.

Several years ago when an appeal was made for churches to adopt Unreached People Groups, a number of churches adopted the Kurds of Turkey, Iran, and Iraq. They began to relate to a strategy coordinator who lived and worked in Berlin among a large expatriate group of Kurdish people. Prior to this, most of these churches had never heard of the Kurds. Then on August 2, 1990, the Gulf War broke out. Iraq invaded Kuwait, the Kurds rose up in revolt against Saddam Hussein, and suddenly this Unreached People Group was in our headlines. The whole region was in upheaval. Relief ministries following the war allowed the gospel to be planted among the Kurds. Several of these churches said they didn't understand what was happening, but they sensed they had been a part of these global events, because of their prayers for the Kurds. They could not have known or determined how their prayers would be answered. Their prayers may not have brought about the Gulf War, but God knew what was going to happen, and they had the privilege of being a part of it!

In 1994 Harps Crossing Baptist Church in Fayetteville, Georgia, adopted an unreached Muslim people group in China. For two years the church had been praying for a people group to adopt. A number had been considered, but they were finally led to this particular group where there was not yet a missionary assigned. The church was informed that no one was working with these people, and the only way they could be reached was through churches praying for them. Dennis Watson, the pastor, told his congregation that if these people were to enter the kingdom of God it would be necessary for the church to pray them into the kingdom. He said, "We may be making a 25- or 50-year commitment, but it is up to us."

There were prayers lifted for this people group in every worship service and church event. Families among the church membership committed to pray for them. While participating in a missions conference at the church, I was being shown the church facilities. As we walked through the children's wing, the pastor pointed out the maps of China and pictures of Chinese people on the wall. He said, "We are teaching our children to pray for the . . . (and named the people group)." Then tears came into his eyes as he said, "I believe when God opens these people's hearts to the gospel, these boys and girls will be the missionaries that He calls to reap the harvest."

He realized prayer wasn't just a means to obligate God to do something. It was the means by which his people would be on mission with God. There was no doubt in his mind that God would reach that people group. But because Harps Crossing was praying for them, they were the ones God would call and use to accomplish His purpose. They began to research their adopted people. Several volunteer prayer teams began to go to China from the church and pray in the midst of their adopted people. During the past 10 years the church has sent 27 teams to work among the people. A strategy coordinator emerged and several short-term missionaries became available from the church to implement an educational platform to teach English and share the gospel. A volunteer on the first team has now returned as a career missionary.

Is this not the way Paul and Barnabas were sent out as missionaries? They did not walk the aisle at invitation time surrendering to full-time service, telling the church God had called them to go as missionaries. No, the church was fasting and praying, and God revealed they were to send out Paul and Barnabas for the work to which God had called them (Acts 13:2). If churches would begin to pray for the nations and Unreached People Groups, it is not unlikely God would call out the missionaries He needs for the task from within those congregations.

Most churches have never had a missionary called out of their congregation. Could that reflect the fact that the church does not demonstrate a heart for the world, that it isn't burdened and praying for the nations? We considered it "Bold Mission Thrust" when Southern Baptists finally had more than 5,000 overseas missionaries. But that represents such a miniscule number relative to the needs of a lost world. Why don't more people hear God's call? Why are so few stirred in their hearts for the unreached peoples of the world, most of whom don't even have an opportunity to hear of Jesus?

I received a letter from a man in Texas who explained that he was a former pastor who, for health reasons, had to retire early from the ministry. Since retirement he has started a prayer ministry and spends several hours a day in prayer. He explained that he prays regularly for the International Mission Board and for me. He receives the materials from our prayer office and prays systematically for our missionaries. His letter went on to say how burdened he feels about the need for more missionary personnel. He had heard stories of people groups who had no one to come and share the gospel with them. He explained that whenever he prayed he would always link his prayers with a Scripture, and he had been praying Matthew 9:38, "Therefore beseech the Lord of the harvest to send out workers into His harvest." Then he concluded by asking, "Dr. Rankin, why isn't God answering my prayer? Why isn't He calling out the laborers that are needed around the world?"

I wasn't sure how to answer him. I had been wondering the same thing myself. Later I read an article that provided the answer. It quoted a nineteenth century missions advocate who observed that God is calling out the laborers, but the laborers are not responding because of a closed mind, a calloused heart, or a reluctant will.

Why does God tell us to pray for Him to send out the laborers? Isn't God the One who calls? Isn't He capable of stirring the hearts of those He calls to go as missionaries without our help? Yes, but just maybe, we are the ones He wants to hear that call. And just maybe, our church is the one He wants to use to get the job done. When we pray for a lost world and our hearts become burdened for the peoples and nations in darkness, our closed minds become open to the possibilities of how God can use us. Our calloused and self-centered hearts are softened and broken for those who have no opportunity to know Jesus. Our reluctant wills become submissive, and we are willing to say, "Here am I, Lord; send me."

We are told to beseech the Lord of the harvest so that we might become the answer to those prayers. We are not told to pray in order to get God to do what we want done. It is all about entering into a relationship with God and talking with Him to the point that we begin to feel His heartbeat and bring our lives into conformity with what He is doing and what He desires to have done.

In my years as president of the IMB, I have gained an awesome sense of God's providence. It is thrilling to be in a position that gets an overview of how God is working all over the world. It was humbling to realize that He doesn't need Jerry Rankin. He doesn't need the International Mission Board, and He doesn't need Southern Baptists. He is God, and His purpose will be fulfilled. But how tragic if we should be unfaithful to His calling, neglect participating in what He is doing, and forfeit the privilege of joining Him to fulfill His mission! Prayer is the means by which we connect with the heart of God, discern His will, and find our place in His missions task. It is not a precursor or a mere component of missions strategy; it **IS** the strategy!

PERSONALIZED PRAYER FOR
MISSIONARY PERSONNEL

Ask missionaries what their greatest need is, and their reply will always be, "Prayer!" Regardless of their field of assignment, missionary personnel could enumerate many obvious needs, including additional missionary reinforcements and more ministry funds for their work. Most of them live in challenging, cross-cultural situations that require an austere lifestyle. They could easily say their greatest need is a more comfortable home, better sanitation, social outlets for their family, or a more secure environment. They could mention better relationships with national co-workers and their missions team or to see a spiritual breakthrough and a harvest emerge among their people group. The needs are endless, but they realize God is the source and provision for every need.

When God's people unite their hearts in prayer, they are acknowledging a need for something they cannot provide themselves. When they intercede in agreement for the multiplicity of needs on the mission field, their prayers transcend the distance, flow through the heart of God, open the portals of His grace, and connect with the missionary in real time.

For many years Southern Baptists have faithfully followed various versions of a prayer calendar, listing missionaries according to their birthdays. Though they may not know the missionaries or what their particular needs are, they lift their names to the Father in intercession. There is confidence that God, who knows their needs, will bless them in a special way. Missionaries often testify of a breakthrough in outreach to their community, an unusual response to their witness, or a family need being met on that day when thousands of people interceded on their behalf.

While attending a missions conference, I heard one of our personnel asked if anything special had happened on his birthday when people were praying for him. He said, "No," and proceeded to describe a horrible day when everything seemed to go wrong. He had an accident, his generator failed while trying to show a film, and a leak in the plumbing flooded their house. But he said, "I am so glad that you were praying for me on that day as it is no telling how disastrous it could have been otherwise!"

It is wonderful that so many Southern Baptists are conscientious about faithfully praying for missionaries on their birthdays once a year. But more and more personnel cannot be listed on a prayer calendar identifying them as missionaries. They serve in restricted countries through legitimate roles that allow them access to the people and provide a witness where it would not otherwise be possible. But it would have severe consequences for their names to appear on a published list, or on the Internet, identifying them as missionaries. It could result in their having to forfeit their ministry and witness among those who have been deprived of hearing the gospel. They would likely lose their platform—their basis for being in the country—and be deported. Worse still, it could jeopardize their safety and even the lives of local believers with whom they are associating.

Currently more than 40 percent of the personnel serving overseas with the International Mission Board are in places where they cannot be identified as missionaries. Creative strategies have emerged in recent years, enabling them to take the gospel to closed countries and Unreached People Groups. As a generic identification these places are called the Last Frontier because they literally represent the last frontier of the Great Commission being completed. Sometimes these missionaries are listed only by their initials or first name without a specific location being identified. This is frustrating to traditional prayer intercessors, accustomed to knowing for whom they are praying and where they serve. But God knows exactly who those initials represent, where they are, and what their needs are that day. He even knows missionaries serving in the Last Frontier who have birthdays that may not be listed on the prayer calendar at all, and He will hear and answer the prayers of faithful prayer warriors who intercede without even knowing for whom they are praying.

But it is so much more effective for those praying to know the missionaries and their needs and lift them to the Lord faithfully every day. It is important that every missionary have a base of prayer support. Churches are encouraged to adopt missionaries and pray for them regularly and often, not just once a year on their birthdays. Missionaries make a commitment to communicate with the church, share the needs of their family and their work, and report what God is doing where they serve. When it comes time for the Lottie Moon Christmas Offering®, "their adopted missionary" shares personally what the offering means to his or her work. The Cooperative Program allocation from the church is seen as a channel for support of their missionary even as it is dispersed to underwrite the support of the denomination and other missionaries all over the world.

These personalized relationships enable missionaries in Last Frontier assignments to share where they are serving and communicate sensitive needs that could never be published. The churches understand the security precautions and can handle prayer requests discreetly. Many churches have adopted multiple missionary families, sometimes leading every Sunday School department or class to adopt missionaries, communicate with them, encourage them, and intercede on their behalf.

Prayer support is so important that approval for missionary appointment is contingent upon each missionary candidate enlisting at least a hundred intercessors who will covenant to pray for them every day. Currently personnel are being encouraged to initiate a personalized relationship with at least five churches that will adopt them and commit to pray for them. Just as it would be unthinkable to send missionaries to the field and not assure them of financial support, it is irresponsible to allow them to go overseas into Satan's territory without assurance of prayer support. That is even more critical.

Keep praying for missionaries on their birthdays as you get to pray for more than 5,000 missionary personnel all over the world. But far more valuable than calling the name of an anonymous person before the Lord once a year is to adopt a family or individual. Intercede knowledgeably for them. Ask God's blessings on their children. Pray for their housing situation and their neighborhood, for one who may be sick, and for their churches and national co-workers. Pray for their people group and receive periodic updates of how God is answering and blessing their ministry. It is an extremely gratifying experience.

Missionary families have many personal needs, but usually their priority concerns are the people they are trying to reach. When you intercede for missionaries, pray that God will give them wisdom in planning their work and developing mission strategies. Pray for boldness in witnessing as Paul requested in Ephesians 6:19, "and pray on my behalf, that utterance may be given to me in the opening of my mouth, to make known with boldness the mystery of the gospel." Ask for hearts to be softened and responsive, or for a "man of peace," that person of influence who could go before them and open doors of opportunity, dispelling the opposition they would otherwise encounter. One primary result of intercession is the removal of barriers—religious prejudice, opposition, government and community restrictions, threats, and communication obstacles—as they seek to share Christ in a new and unfamiliar language.

Only after these priority issues would most personnel acknowledge their personal and family needs. Their own walk with the Lord is something that cannot be assumed. Demanding schedules, responsibilities for family, and mere survival in an isolated, cross-cultural setting infringe on time needed for spiritual nurture and refreshing. Many do not have a local church that feeds and ministers to them as they reach out and disciple new believers in infant congregations. Protection and health cannot be taken for granted where traffic congestion, chaotic driving patterns, and unsanitary conditions are the norm. The education and social needs of children—and the difficulty of separation as they go to boarding school or return to the States for college—are at the top of many missionaries' prayer lists.

Pray also for relationships with colleagues. Conflicts and strained interpersonal relationships erode effectiveness and add a burden that robs one of joy and fulfillment. It is not only our missionaries, those whom we know and love, who need our prayers, but the pastors and lay evangelists with whom they work. These saints face persecution and suffering for their faith far beyond that which is usually encountered by expatriate missionaries.

The Bible instructs us to pray for kings and those in authority. We need to pray for the country where the missionary serves and for the government leaders. Pray for visas and work permits to be granted and renewed without undue bureaucratic hassles. Pray for a hedge of protection against illness and danger. Pray for fluency in the language and that God will grant favorable relationships as they seek to identify with the people. The list is endless. God knows the needs of missionaries. But it is much more gratifying and effective to be able to enter into the life and ministry of a missionary through knowledgeable, personalized praying.

PRAYERPLUS PARTNERSHIPS

Just as churches adopt missionaries and pray for them, churches and individuals can adopt the people group with whom missionaries are working or an unreached group that is yet to be engaged with the gospel. Testimonies are abundant of an evangelistic breakthrough after a people group has become the focus of a church's prayer. Like the experience of Harps Crossing Baptist Church, sometimes missionaries are called out to meet the need and be the answer to the church's prayers.

This is called a PRAYERPlus Partnership. A church makes a commitment to partner with the International Mission Board by praying for an Unreached People Group, recognizing that prayer is the foundational missions strategy. Prayer is something everyone can do. The church can take ownership of a strategy to reach a people on the other side of the world without ever going there. It doesn't cost a thing, nor does it necessarily infringe on an already over-committed budget. However, there is a contingency—the "plus." It is a commitment to pray, plus a commitment to do whatever God leads the church to do in response to praying.

God may lead the church to enlist volunteer personnel to actually travel to where the people group is located and intercede for them on-site. He may give members the privilege of providing materials and resources needed to penetrate the people group with the gospel, such as underwriting the production of the *JESUS* film in their language, sponsoring a radio broadcast, publishing and distributing tracts and Scripture portions. It will not be the International Mission Board making such requests. It will be God leading; as the church prays, He will reveal what He wants done as He reveals how He is working.

Can you imagine the thrill of one day gathering around the throne of God and finding there a group of Beja from the Sudan or Wolof from Senegal included in that gathering because you and your church prayed them into the kingdom?

When disability and early retirement forced him to slow down, Tom Wright felt God speaking to him about a commitment he had made as a child. One Sunday morning Tom hobbled down the aisle and devoted himself to intercessory prayer for his church. The pastor had recently asked the congregation to pray for an Unreached People Group in the Last Frontier. Tom took the lead on the project. He promoted prayer for them, he prayed long hours for them himself, and he always asked prayer for them whenever the church met. They became his people.

A year went by and Tom expanded his prayer for the people group. He felt led to pray that the *JESUS* film be translated into their language. One of his fellow church members told him: "Tom, you can pray for that, but I have seen the websites on this people group. Only the old people and the priests speak that language now. No one else does. I think it would be a waste of time." But Tom and the church were persistent in their prayers.

Two years later, a couple living and working among the people group came to the church and gave a report. They told how four years before there were no known believers among the group and little response to the gospel. But three years ago, they said, things changed. It was sudden and dramatic. The International Mission Board sent workers to live among them and they began to respond. Now there were more than 500 believers. Tom realized this was about the time of his struggle with God. It was also about the time his pastor asked the congregation to begin praying for this people group and Tom had taken them on as a project.

The two workers went on to report that not having Scripture in the heart language of the people was one of the big problems for this group. While everyone spoke the language common to the country, in their homes and among themselves they still spoke the traditional language of their ancestors. But there was hope, they said. Two years before, one of the new believers felt called to translate the *JESUS* film into their language and was about to complete it.

The timing was more than coincidence. The man was called after Tom began to pray for that translation. The church was moved as they realized the Lord had brought the missionaries who live among their people group, love them, and know them, to their church to show how He was answering their prayers.

Most of our kingdom praying is for the missionaries we know and who go out from our churches. That is appropriate, but the real focus of our intercession should be on the peoples of the world who need to know Jesus. We need to realize, though, that to pray for peoples in darkness means engaging in warfare against powers and principalities. The Apostle Paul indicated a clear understanding of the missionary task when he testified in Acts 26:16–18 that God had called him as a witness to the Gentiles . . . "to open their eyes so that they may turn from darkness to light and from the dominion of Satan to God." He recognized that the task of missions was one of spiritual warfare, and which includes our intercessory praying.

Missionaries are literally venturing into Satan's territory—the peoples, countries, and cultures that do not know Jesus Christ are literally the domain of Satan. The people who dwell in these lands are in bondage to principalities and the prince of the air. They do not know there is anything other than the fears and superstitions with which they have lived all their lives. As one new believer in a Last Frontier country said after hearing and responding to the gospel, "When you are born in the darkness and live your life in the darkness, you never know there is Light."

Having served in the largest Muslim country in the world, I quickly discovered that expecting a Muslim to respond to the gospel is like asking a blind man to read a newspaper. Second Corinthians 4:3–4 says, "even if our gospel is veiled, it is veiled to those who are perishing, in whose case the god of this world has blinded the minds of the unbelieving, that they might not see the light of the gospel of the glory of Christ."

Our missionaries are dealing with an enemy that is powerful and deceitful. Not only must we pray for an anointing of power and discernment on their part, we also need to pray against the strongholds of Satan. They hold people in bondage to sin and false religions which only leads to destruction. In the account of the temptations of Jesus in Luke 4:5–6 we read: "And he led Him up and showed Him all the kingdoms of the world in a moment of time. And the devil said to Him, 'I will give You all this domain and its glory; for it has been handed over to me, and I give it to whomever I wish.'" Of course Jesus did not succumb to that temptation, even though all the kingdoms of the world becoming the kingdom of God was what His coming was all about. But it would happen, not in response to Satan's deceit, but only as He gave His life on the cross and rose again to conquer the sins of the world. However, it is intriguing that Jesus did not contradict the devil's claim to possess the kingdoms of the world. 1 John 5:19 says, "We are of God, and the whole world lies in the power of the evil one."

So, how do we claim the nations and peoples of the world for Christ and enable them to become a part of His kingdom? James 4:2 tells us that "(We) do not have because (we) do not ask." We are reminded of all the amazing prayer promises throughout the Scripture when we ask in accordance with the Father's will and make our requests consistent with that which will glorify Him. Surely kingdom growth fits that category. We have already seen how God's heart and desire is to be exalted among the nations, but how much do we pray in that regard? Remember that awesome promise in Psalm 2:8 that God, who is sovereign over the nations, will enable them to become His possession contingent on our praying for them.

Few churches and individuals have ventured into true kingdom praying, beseeching God for the nations and peoples of the world. Is it any wonder that 2,000 years after our Lord told us to proclaim good news of the kingdom to the ends of the earth, more than 30 percent of the world has not even heard that Christ died for them? Is it any wonder that so many peoples remain unreached, living in despair, in bondage to the power of sin, with no hope?

On a recent trip overseas I had the privilege of spending the day with a group of strategy coordinators. It was thrilling to hear some of them describe what their teams were doing, to hear testimonies of the first church being planted, or how the gospel was multiplying and churches beginning to grow. Others had not yet had a breakthrough but were optimistic as they shared their visions and reviewed their plans. By midafternoon the group had moved into a prayer time in which they prayed for each other and the challenges they were facing. They interceded for colleagues who were having health problems, for families who had had to return to the States, and for the gap it had left on their team. They prayed for local pastors and the various ministries that were building relationships and providing opportunities for witness. I learned more just listening to the prayers that were voiced than from the earlier reports.

The prayers soon moved into intercession for the peoples and cities to which these missionaries were assigned. Most of these strategy coordinators were no longer kneeling at their chairs but were prostrate on the floor. It became difficult for them to fluently voice their prayers due to their emotion and sobbing as they wept for their people.

Is this not what God would want us and our churches to do? It would be impossible to pray systematically for all 11,249 people groups around the world, but if every church would adopt a specific people group and pour out their hearts on behalf of them, the barriers would vanish, doors would open, Satan's strongholds would crumble, and the power of the gospel would begin to bring people into God's kingdom.

How will this come about? It may be the people group with which a missionary acquaintance is working. Or it may be one where no one has yet been assigned, and because of your prayers, the Lord of the harvest would call out and send laborers into a new field to plant the gospel. Because of your prayers the government may be changed and restrictions eased. A natural disaster may open the door for an incarnational witness by Christian humanitarian workers. An expatriate immigrant from that people group may actually surface in your city or community! God's ways are not our ways, but He has chosen to work in accord with the prayers of His people.

Prayerwalking and Providential Impact

It is unclear when and how the concept of prayerwalking began. When Joshua and the men of Israel entered the Promised Land, the Lord told them to claim all the land where they walked. In recent years prayerwalking has emerged as a phenomenon that is making a powerful impact on a lost world. Certainly we can pray anytime, anywhere. The God of the universe hears and honors our prayers of intercession for others, even on the opposite side of the world. Recognizing prayer as a foundational strategy, missionaries more and more began to walk the streets of their neighborhoods, praying for the people they casually encountered. They prayed for those who lived in the crowded apartment blocks they passed and for those who worked in the stores and businesses. They intentionally scheduled time to go to a high hill or rooftop overlooking their cities to intercede for the masses who did not know Jesus.

As churches in America adopted and prayed for Unreached People Groups with strange-sounding names, a curiosity emerged that led them to want to see and know those for whom they were praying. Their fascination grew as they focused on a modern-day culture that remained isolated geographically in places where the gospel had never been proclaimed. Groups began to go to places where a Christian witness was prohibited to simply pray on-site with greater insight into the lives and needs of their adopted people.

Years ago I remember stories of those who traveled to Eastern Europe to pray with the remnant of persecuted believers and intercede that the Iron Curtain would come down and freedom would come to these nations. There were those praying for an opening and response in the Catholic strongholds of South America. As the vision grew for penetrating Last Frontier nations and people groups, prayer strategies were initially the only option for fulfilling that vision. Intercessors were enlisted to go as tourists and pray as they visited national shrines, government buildings, and while walking through the marketplaces. They would go to university campuses and pray for the students, invoking God's blessings on a people who did not know Him.

Central Asian countries became a primary target of prayerwalking in the early 1990s as the former Soviet Union began to disintegrate. A group of churches had been enlisted to pray for the Azeri people of Azerbaijan, and a consolidated prayer team traveled into the country before there were any known Azeri believers. Today there are 74 churches and more than 3,500 believers.

While attending a conference of personnel in East Asia, I listened to the group share brief testimonies of what was happening in their place of assignment. One young man said he had been sent to an unevangelized city in China where there were not yet any churches. He said, "I have been there a year; now more than 1,500 have been baptized and there are already 30 churches." With that brief comment he sat down. Curious to know how such phenomenal growth could happen, I found him after the session and asked about his strategy and what he had done to produce such results. He seemed unclear and ambiguous about how it had happened, disclaiming any significant personal involvement. Then he added, "Several groups of South Koreans came through our city on prayerwalks last year, and I think that might have had something to do with it!"

When Rob and Nan Sugg, veteran missionaries in Taiwan, moved to Tainan City for a church-planting assignment, they were aware they were entering an especially superstitious, pagan area. They prayed diligently, seeking the Lord's leadership in everything they did. Though they worked hard and tried many approaches, nothing worked. People were unresponsive. Discouraged, they wrote to family, friends, and churches, asking them to pray on their behalf. Those who responded joined them in praying with focused understanding of the needs and challenges in Tainan City.

One day as Nan was reading in Joshua, she felt God telling her to walk around her Jericho seven times if she wanted the walls to come down. Reading Ephesians 6:10–18, she made sure of her spiritual armor and walked the neighborhood, sketching a map of all the roads, lanes, alleys, and houses. She prayed as she went, claiming the area for God and repeated the experience again and again. Rob and Nan felt a sense of oppression due to a Buddhist temple located at the head of their street. As the Suggs continued to pray around the neighborhood, they noticed one day that the temple was being torn down and dismantled. Soon a vibrant new church of 35 believers were worshiping together and sharing their witness throughout the city.

As I travel in countries all over the world I have been conditioned to pray everywhere I go, interceding for the people on the streets. I am reminded that God loves them, Jesus died for them, and they need to know His salvation. I pray over a city as the airplane is landing. I lift up the government leaders, the missionaries, and national Christians who serve God in those places. Wherever I am, I constantly pray Habakkuk 2:14 that "the earth will be filled with the knowledge of the glory of the Lord, as the waters cover the sea."

There are many places throughout the world where one cannot witness openly, pass out tracts, or give out Bibles. One can get arrested for showing the *JESUS* film or gathering openly in a public assembly with believers in some countries. But there is no power on earth that can prevent one from praying. We can pray at home or as we travel overseas, claiming cities, countries, and people groups for our Lord with assurance that one day "every knee will bow . . . and . . . every tongue will confess that Jesus is Lord, to the glory of God the Father" (Philippians 2:10–11).

Everywhere I served in South and Southeast Asia I would observe that some churches and mission groups were growing and flourishing while others seemed to languish, struggling to maintain the status quo. There were many groups that were discouraged and never reflected a vision for evangelism and outreach among difficult and resistant population groups. Yet others were multiplying congregations and reaching large numbers of people. They weren't all Baptist, though some were. Others were clearly Pentecostal or independent Christian missions.

I visited these successful ministries in an effort to discern what made the difference between them and those that were languishing. There was a great deal of diversity in doctrine and worship style, but I found three common threads that characterized each one: (1) They had a burden for the lostness around them and a zeal for witnessing and sharing Jesus that was undeterred by cultural barriers; discretion was not in their vocabulary. (2) They had a bold faith that expected God to work; a faith that was the explanation for what could only be defined as signs and wonders. (3) But finally, they were always people of prayer. They spoke matter-of-factly about all-night prayer and fasting. They gathered for early morning prayer meetings before dawn. Their worship service was punctuated by extended times of intercession, corporate praying, and prayer-centered ministry to individuals.

Acts 4:31 says, "And when they had prayed . . . they were all filled with the Holy Spirit, and began to speak the word of God with boldness." Praying enables us to participate in the providential work of God's Spirit as He moves among the nations, claiming them for His possession. Missionaries and intercessors must be sure they have put on their spiritual armor and are personally equipped for the battle.

We must gird our loins with truth, don the breastplate of righteousness, shod our feet with the preparation of the gospel, wear the helmet of salvation, and wield the sword of the Spirit—but only as it is bathed in prayer. Ephesians 6:18 adds, "With all prayer and petition pray at all times in the Spirit, and with this in view, be on the alert with all perseverance and petition for all the saints."

Will you and your church put on God's armor and persevere in prayer and petition for the missionaries, the people groups, and the nations of the world? Prayer is what enables the Holy Spirit to give boldness to our witness. It unleashes the power of God and changes lives. It is the foundation for empowering kingdom growth.

1. C. H. Spurgeon, "Ask and Have," *Twelve Sermons on Prayer* (Chicago: Fleming H. Revell Company, 188?), 548 and C. H. Spurgeon, "The Waterer Watered," *The Metropolitan Tabernacle Pulpit: Sermons Preached and Revised by C. H. Spurgeon During the Year 1865* (London: Passmore Alabaster, 1866), 236.

CHAPTER FOUR

PLANTING THE SEEDS . . .
REAPING THE HARVEST

IMB BASIC PURPOSE:

Provide all people an opportunity to hear, understand, and respond to the gospel in their own cultural context.

IMB BASIC TASK:

Evangelism through proclamation, discipleship, equipping, and ministry that results in indigenous Baptist churches.

The heat was stifling in the simple, one-room bamboo house crowded with people. A diverse assortment of chairs and every available bench had been gathered from the neighborhood. Children sat cross-legged on straw mats spread over the dirt floor, occupying every available space. The only light was a few tiny, flickering flames of burning wicks protruding from tin cans that had been turned into kerosene lamps. They gave enough light to illuminate the words of my Bible if held close to the page but also reflected the white teeth of smiling faces and sparkling eyes of those seated in the dark corners of the house.

This group had rapidly been growing in their understanding of the claims of Jesus Christ. They sang heartily the simple choruses of praise they had learned, their joy and enthusiasm clearly evident when they shifted from Indonesian to those that had been translated into their more familiar Javanese language. It had been almost two months since I stopped along the roadside to chat with a group of these men as they paused in the heat of the day from working in their rice fields. Their reaction to our initial conversation was a mixture of suspicion and amusement that an American would be in Indonesia and in the vicinity of their remote village in East Java.

Their questions followed the usual progression. "Who are you?" "Where are you from?" "Why are you here?" That final inquiry always set up an opportunity to share my personal testimony. I would talk about knowing God, how much He cared for the people of Indonesia, and my desire to tell them how they could know Him and also have assurance of eternal life. That explanation was often met with antagonism when someone discerned I was seeking to proselytize and impose my Christian beliefs on their Muslim society. The more common response was disinterest and indifference, after which the conversation would revert to the weather or trivial questions about America.

This time, however, one in the group, speaking for the others, said he would very much like to hear about how to receive eternal life. I asked if he believed in God. He replied, as all Indonesians, that he did but did not know Him. He volunteered that, although he faithfully went to the mosque on Friday and quoted the prayers each day, he did not understand Arabic and the Quran had no meaning to him. Further discussion proved to enhance their interest and elicited an invitation to come to their *kampong*—the neighborhood where they and extended family members lived—in the evening.

Not wanting to allow time to elapse and miss following up on this contact, I continued my itinerant probing and witnessing in the area through the afternoon and shortly after sunset found my new friends in the village of Curahnongko. Having bathed and eaten, they were delighted to see me, but had been skeptical that I, as an American, would keep my promise to visit them. The uniqueness of an American visitor in their community attracted considerable attention. Tea was served, and the house was soon packed with giggling children and a crowd of curious men and women. The courtyard filled as news began to spread of the presence of a foreigner.

That first evening was spent getting acquainted as I expressed interest in them and their village and asked questions about their lives and relationships. It resulted in a commitment to return the next week and share the Word of God with them. After several weeks, I had shared every approach I knew to explain the gospel—the Roman Road, John 3:16, the Four Spiritual Laws and others—and satisfactorily answered their questions. I had provided Bibles that I encouraged them to read. Their spiritual sensitivity and inquisitiveness was evident by the questions they asked when I returned each week. I began to pray for them and teach them to pray.

It became more and more apparent they believed all that I was teaching and sharing, and I was able to lead them in individual prayers of commitment to receive Jesus Christ as personal Lord and Savior. I explained that baptism was the scriptural way of testifying of their new faith and publicly acknowledging Jesus, and 26 people affirmed their desire to follow Jesus.

I began to teach them what it meant to be a church and to function as a local body of baptized believers. They were to gather for worship regularly, witness to others, and nurture each other in their understanding and growth of the Christian life. One particular night I made the suggestion that they begin to gather and worship on Sundays. This was clearly known as the day of Christian worship, followed biblical practice, and it would be a testimony of their faith in their Muslim village. I sensed what I thought was a reluctance to try to conduct a worship service when I could not be there to lead them. I tried to convince them that they could sing the songs they had learned, pray as they had been taught, and read the Bible and discuss what it said and how it applied to their lives without my being present. Two or three of the men were already demonstrating spiritual sensitivity and leadership skills. I assured them the Holy Spirit would enlighten their understanding as they read the Bible in faith and shared their understanding of what it meant.

The group seemed confused by my efforts to persuade them to gather on Sunday when I could come only on Tuesday. Finally, one of them said, "We are already doing what you are suggesting on Sunday, and also on Monday, Tuesday, Wednesday, Thursday, Friday, and Saturday. Now that we are a church, are we just to gather on Sunday?"

I was startled by this information. Acts 5:42 immediately came to mind. We are told of the early believers in Jerusalem, that "... every day, in the temple and from house to house, they kept right on teaching and preaching Jesus as the Christ." Immediately God impressed me that I was not to impose traditional forms and structures from our Western model and cultural practice of what a church is, but was to allow the Holy Spirit to guide local believers in a way that would be consistent with the New Testament expression of the church.

One of the men who was clearly respected had already begun to step into the role of primary pastoral leadership. As this church in Curahnongko quickly assumed responsibility for their worship, my visits became more infrequent. Each time I worshiped with them, I met other new believers who had joined the group and had been baptized. They often told of going to neighboring villages, leading Bible studies, and sharing what they themselves had learned. My continuing contact with this church, and many similar new churches in my area of assignment in Indonesia, became one of meeting with the leaders to train and nurture them in their pastoral roles and to deepen their knowledge and understanding of the Bible.

CHURCH PLANTING—OUR BASIC TASK

The purpose of the International Mission Board is to provide all people an opportunity to hear, understand, and respond to the gospel in their own cultural context. We cannot do anything to bring about conversion. It is only the regenerating work of the Holy Spirit that can bring one to faith in Jesus Christ and bring about a genuine experience of being born again in response to our witness and proclamation. That is why we often declare that we are not interested in proselytizing, for it does no good for someone to simply change from one religion to another. It is not religion that saves.

When someone says all religions are the same, he is right. It really doesn't matter which one someone chooses to follow. Teaching the tenets of religious beliefs and embracing them intellectually is meaningless with regard to salvation. Only a personal, saving relationship with Jesus Christ that comes through one's repentance and faith can make a difference. That is the power of the gospel.

Evangelism—proclaiming the gospel and making it known—is the heart of a missionary's work. That does not mean that every missionary is a preacher. But regardless of the assignment, the gospel is to be shared verbally and lived out in relationships and in holistic ministry. Every means possible that enables us to relate to a lost world, win a credible hearing, and elicit a response can and should be used. That includes education, health care, hunger relief, disaster response, and compassionate pastoral care. Missionaries go to proclaim the gospel and make it known to a lost world. Yet it is not what they do but the power of the Holy Spirit that convicts people of sin, of the truth of the gospel, and draws people to Christ.

The challenge we face is to proclaim the gospel to all the people in the world. Although 33 percent of the world's population are identified as Christians, most are cultural Christians with no understanding of a personal faith in Jesus Christ. Research reveals that about 10 percent of the world's population are born-again believers. That is about 600 million out of a global population now in excess of 6 billion. One out of 10 is remarkable and should make the task of evangelizing the world something that could readily be accomplished. However, the problem is one of proportion. Most of the evangelical Christian

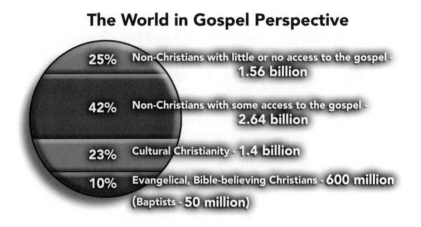

The World in Gospel Perspective

25%	Non-Christians with little or no access to the gospel - **1.56 billion**
42%	Non-Christians with some access to the gospel - **2.64 billion**
23%	Cultural Christianity - **1.4 billion**
10%	Evangelical, Bible-believing Christians - **600 million** (Baptists - **50 million**)

population is concentrated in America and a few other evangelized countries, leaving vast population segments around the world with no access to a church or Christian witness.

Southern Baptists now have more than 5,000 international missionaries across the globe, but that represents only one missionary unit for every 1.2 million people. It would be an awesome challenge for a single missionary or family to be responsible for personally reaching 1.2 million people—each one's approximate proportion of the lost population.

The church-planting experience I related above was in the context of my wife and me being the only missionaries in an area of 5.5 million people. The result of our witness was a group of baptized local believers, drawn together by the Holy Spirit into a visible fellowship for worship and witness as a New Testament church. This covenant community became a nucleus of witness and ministry, reaching beyond what we as individual missionaries could do.

Because the church is indwelt by the Holy Spirit as the body of Christ, it is natural for it to grow numerically through an expanding witness and to multiply by planting other new churches. As these local, indigenous churches reproduce and replicate themselves, they become an expanding network that can literally make the gospel accessible to the whole world. The end of evangelism is not just to witness to others, or even to lead others to a decision of accepting Christ. It includes discipling new believers and incorporating them into a local, nurturing fellowship of believers.

I'll never forget one of our annual gatherings of missionaries. We always anticipated this annual meeting and the opportunity to be with colleagues we seldom saw due to our isolated assignment. The program was filled with inspirational worship and testimonies of what God was doing throughout the country. Generally the reports focused on how many new believers had been baptized and new churches started. But in the midst of talk about new converts and churches someone asked, "How many disciples did you make this year?" This challenging new question was met with a startled response of silence. We all immediately recognized the validity of the question.

Jesus had commissioned us to make disciples, but how does one respond to that with confidence and credibility? We could count the number of baptisms, but how many of them were truly living for Christ and gave evidence of becoming a Christ-like follower of the Master in faith and obedience? I began to squirm as I immediately thought of some of the new Christians in my area. They were apparently converts of Jerry Rankin—they had answered all the right questions—but were struggling in their newfound faith. Their character formation still had a long way to go; I wasn't sure I was ready to identify them as "disciples."

Missiologist Donald McGavran interpreted "making disciples" as the conversion experience, after which new believers were to be "perfected" through teaching and nurturing. However, we generally understand discipling as that process of growth in understanding and obedience which follows the salvation experience. While we rejoice in the millions of people responding to a Christian witness around the world, the IMB does not track or report "professions of faith." Whether immediately after that decision or following an initial period of teaching, water baptism is regarded as the scriptural form of confessing one's faith. It is that public step that clearly identifies a new believer. It demonstrates that one has put aside former beliefs and religious adherence to be a follower of Jesus Christ.

We rejoice in all who respond to a passing witness of a missions volunteer or multitudes who may indicate their desire to follow Christ in response to a public invitation at a massive crusade. Only God can know the level of understanding and what has transpired in the heart of one who lifts his hand or prays a prayer of confession. But total evangelism is lacking without follow-up. Unless a new believer is incorporated into a church fellowship, the step of discipleship is incomplete. Converts may have assurance of eternal life, but it is the Christlike learners and followers of Jesus who continue to grow in their faith. The kingdom growth occurs only as new believers witness to their neighbors and family, faithfully worship with fellow believers, and join in ministering to the needs around them. Jesus sent us not just to proclaim the gospel of salvation but the gospel of the kingdom. It is a message of redemption through which individuals are born again, but the result is the Lordship and reign of Christ in the lives of His people.

This aspect of our mission task is clearly reflected in the accountability of missionaries and the annual statistical report of the IMB. In 2003 there were 600,807 baptisms recorded. Of that number 490,046 new believers were reported to have participated in discipleship training. Of the total membership of 7,357,986 for churches related to IMB work overseas, almost 4 million participated in Sunday School, Bible teaching ministries, or discipleship training outside the primary worship service.

Evangelism that results in churches is the kind of evangelism that makes disciples. We should preach the gospel to every creature, seek to persuade and win every individual, but our mission must never be less than what Jesus told us to do—to make disciples of all nations and peoples.

We have all seen the potential of exponential growth through witnessing and how quickly the world can be won. It depends upon everyone leading someone else to Christ each year, and each one of those in turn winning others consistently. But the formula breaks down because many won to Christ never become witnesses and because so many of the lost—especially among Unreached People Groups—are beyond access to a Christian witness. Most of the lost of the world live in places where there are no churches and no Christians.

There will never be enough cross-cultural missionaries to touch all the people in the world with a witness that will enable them to hear, understand, and respond to the gospel in their own cultural contexts. But when our cross-cultural witness results in a church, there is a permanent, ongoing nucleus of witness in a community. This witness extends the evangelistic effort beyond the occasional visit of an itinerant missionary or volunteer team. And because it is the nature of a church—indwelt of God's Spirit—to grow and multiply, a network of reproducing indigenous congregations can eventually envelop a town, a district, a province, a country, and people group, making the gospel accessible to everyone.

CHURCH-PLANTING MOVEMENTS (CPMs)

The objective of a church-planting strategy of evangelism is not just an increase in the number of churches. It is to facilitate a rapid reproduction of churches, making the gospel available so that lost people everywhere can come to saving faith in Christ. Planting new churches is the surest way to increase the number of believers, but missionaries themselves cannot produce a rapid multiplication of new churches. It is contingent upon churches starting churches. The churches themselves must catch the vision of the missionary or national church planter to extend their witness and nurture believers in another location.

There is a spiritual element in the DNA of a new church to share its faith in an expanded witness and start other churches from the very beginning. One church starts another. Two churches become four, four become eight, and eight become 16 in rapid, exponential multiplication.

In one country where Baptists have caught the vision of church-planting movements, mission points cannot be recognized as an organized, member church of the convention until they have already started another mission. In a Latin American country the number of churches increased from 654 in 1995 to more than 5,000 by 2002, and the number of members grew sevenfold.

In India there were 24 Baptist churches among a people group numbering 90 million. No new church had been started in 25 years because they had been focused on a model that was dependent on outsiders contributing resources to provide a building and support their pastors. When these subsidies were discontinued, they ceased to grow. But then they began to get a renewed fervor for evangelism through the training and influence of a missionary. They began to realize the biblical and spiritual nature of a church was neither con-tingent on a full-time, seminary-trained pastor nor on special facili-ties. New congregations of believers began to emerge and multiply. During the next year 58 new churches were started. Three years later there were 1,200 churches, which then more than tripled in the fol-lowing two years. As of 2000 there were more than 4,000 Baptist churches among this people group. These churches are not just small cells of two or three believers or an extended family meeting together for worship. A recent research report indicated baptized members meeting regularly for worship averaged more than 60 in each church.

One of my most thrilling experiences in my overseas travels was the privilege of visiting Cambodia for the first time. It was right after the fifth annual meeting of the Cambodian Baptist Convention. At the time, they reported 243 churches with more than 16,000 baptized members. None of the churches was led by missionaries. In fact, for foreigners to even attend the churches would have jeopardized their security in this communist country.

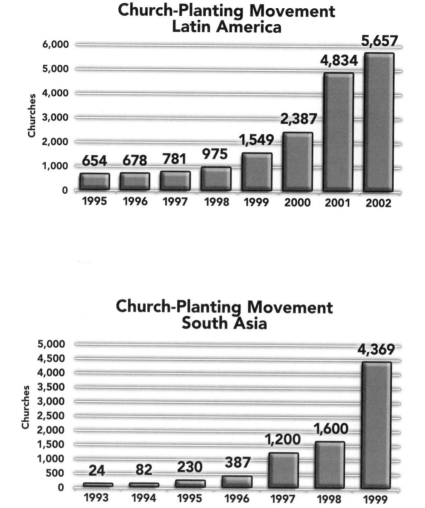

Church-Planting Movement
Latin America

Churches

6,000
5,000
4,000
3,000
2,000
1,000
0

654 **678** **781** **975** **1,549** **2,387** **4,834** **5,657**

1995 1996 1997 1998 1999 2000 2001 2002

Church-Planting Movement
South Asia

Churches

5,000
4,500
4,000
3,500
3,000
2,500
2,000
1,500
1,000
500
0

24 **82** **230** **387** **1,200** **1,600** **4,369**

1993 1994 1995 1996 1997 1998 1999

The missionaries engaged in humanitarian projects and poured themselves into discipling and training lay leaders who not only led their own congregations but started others. I attended one of the quarterly, two-week training sessions attended by 20 lay pastors. Most of them had been believers less than two years. Each reported pastoring at least two churches—one pastored six—and all of them had projected locations for starting new churches as soon as their training was finished.

Church-planting movements are taking place throughout China as house-church networks multiply in phenomenal numbers. Already three such networks report 18 million to 20 million members, each one larger than the Southern Baptist Convention. An IMB strategy coordinator went to a province with three churches in 1993, and by 1998 there were 550 churches.

The IMB is tracking about 80 existing and potential church-planting movements throughout the world. Many more are beginning to emerge. It is one reason incremental growth reported in the past has turned into church growth rates of more than 20 percent a year. In 2001, 8,379 new churches were started. That grew to more than 16,600 the following year, and 21,028 were started in 2003. This is not an aberration or a short-lived peak in church planting. In addition to these new churches, 50,297 additional mission points and outreach groups that are not yet churches are being reported.

This pace of new church growth was the primary factor in being able to report more than 600,000 new believers baptized overseas for the first time in the history of the International Mission Board. New churches invariably grow faster and reach more people than older, established churches. Some would raise the question about what is being reported as a church. A church is a group of baptized believers covenanted together into community by the Holy Spirit for the purpose of worship, fellowship, witness, nurture, and ministry.

A local church is a group of baptized believers covenanted together into community by the Holy Spirit for the purpose of worship, fellowship, witness, nurture, and ministry. The following characteristics are considered when completing the statistical report:

1. Meet regularly for worship, fellowship, mutual support, and ministry.

2. **Proclaim Christ to unbelievers and disciple believers.**

3. **Organize and administer their affairs, choose their leadership (who may or may not be paid, trained, ordained, or one of the members of the group).**

4. **Administer the ordinances of baptism and the Lord's Supper.**

In order to have a rapid multiplication of churches, they must be indigenous. They cannot be dependent on outside finances and leadership. From the beginning they must be self-supporting, self-governing under the Lordship of Christ, and self-propagating in extending their witness. They practice an expression of organization and worship that is consistent with biblical teaching but in their own cultural context.

Most churches in America would not serve as models for indigenous churches in overseas cultures. Churches in other cultures built on Western models seldom multiply and usually cannot even survive unless someone props them up with an artificial system of support. There is a lesson in landscaping that illustrates this. I would like to have palm trees and tropical shrubs in my yard in Virginia such as I enjoyed in Indonesia and sometimes see when I go to Florida. But because they are not indigenous to my part of the country, they would not survive on their own apart from a greenhouse environment.

Scripture and worship should always be in the heart language of the people. It eliminates cross-cultural and language barriers to worship and hearing the gospel, allowing the church to multiply within a homogeneous people group. Churches that multiply rapidly usually have bivocational lay pastors and leaders. They emerge from within the congregation and give evidence of spiritual gifts and sensitivity for leadership roles. They are not limited by lack of financial support or prescribed educational standards. They can readily train others, multiplying the leadership that is needed. However, the rapid evangelistic growth does not necessarily happen because of leaders. New believers enthusiastically sharing their faith person-to-person, wherever they can, are the real catalysts, though the movement often starts by the gospel being introduced the first time by a Western or national missionary.

Church-planting movements are taking place among previously Unreached People Groups, even where there are restrictions on preaching, conducting public worship, and witnessing. There are many testimonies where an evangelist or missionary has found a "man of peace" as Jesus instructed His disciples when He sent them out in Luke 10. This is a person of influence who is an important contact in the community who may or may not himself become a believer. But he opens the door to relationships that allow the gospel to be shared.

It is important that the initial witness and the first churches started not only be indigenous but firmly grounded on the authority of the Bible and priesthood of all believers. Media missionaries working outside the country have often played a vital role in saturating the area with gospel radio broadcasts and providing the *JESUS* film in forms that can be distributed and shared from household to household. One remote area in a restricted, closed country has seen 1,800 believers come to Christ during the past five years through literature and video packets strategically dropped throughout the area. These brick-sized packets, containing the *JESUS* film, a New Testament in the local language, and other evangelistic literature, were found and passed from family to family and house to house. The villagers talked about what they had seen and read. They not only believed but shared it in a widespread witness.

Strategies like this are often implemented among people groups where a missionary cannot live. After discovering ways for planting the gospel and saturation witness, the role of an external missionary becomes one of nurturing the movement. This is done by providing leadership training, conducting workshops on evangelism and discipleship, and mobilizing prayer support.

In places where it is possible to live among the people—or at least visit the area periodically—the missionary follows a four-step approach of modeling, assisting, watching, and leaving. He may lead the first group of believers for a few weeks, but will lead in such a way that a local leader can assume that responsibility. After receiving encouragement, training, and assistance for a short time, the local leader can imitate the method and pass on the training to other lay pastors and evangelists. Relinquishing all leadership roles, the missionary stays in contact, watching and advising as needed before leaving and moving on to other unevangelized areas.

The reluctance to relinquish leadership early in the process has been one of the primary weaknesses of traditional church-planting efforts. Once the missionary is seen and accepted as the primary leader, it is awkward, if not impossible, to pass on that role to an untrained local leader within the group. The alternative is for the new church to look for a pastor from without, imposing another factor detrimental to its strength and vitality and impeding its ability to grow and multiply spontaneously and independently.

On Paul's first missionary journey he spent only two or three weeks in each city proclaiming the gospel. As he reversed the circuit, we read in Acts 14:23, "And when they had appointed elders for them in every church, having prayed with fasting, they commended them to the Lord in whom they had believed." They ordained or set apart these relatively new believers to lead the churches. They didn't select these men as elders because they had confidence in them, but because they had confidence in the Lord, in whom they had trusted for guidance. God had revealed to Paul that the Holy Spirit would disperse the gifts needed within each local body for its completion and perfection. Growth of the church is often inhibited by failure to trust God to raise up the leaders and failure to nurture gifts within the body.

Church-planting movements cannot occur when there is a dependency on an outsider to fulfill the responsibilities of leadership.

Another missionary has identified the principles for nurturing church-planting movements with the acrostic, "POUCH." This stands for (1) **P**articipative Bible study and worship, (2) **O**bedience to God's Word, (3) **U**npaid and multiple lay leaders, (4) **C**ell churches that rapidly divide and multiply, and (5) **H**omes as the primary meeting place within a community where outsiders feel welcome.

Most missionaries who have had a role in seeing church-planting movements among their assigned people group were committed to the admonition of 2 Timothy 2:2: "And the things which you have heard from me in the presence of many witnesses, entrust these to faithful men, who will be able to teach others also." They never do anything alone, but are always modeling for national believers the vision, skills, and methods of witnessing, discipling, training, and their own personal walk with the Lord.

As the movement expands, it is imperative to set up training programs and extension centers of basic theological education. It becomes impossible to continue one-on-one training as the number of leaders multiplies exponentially. Since it does not create local church dependency, assistance in funding and support for these training programs is often necessary. This is a high priority of the IMB, and more than 120,000 grass-roots leaders participated in training modules and courses in 2003.

However, the continuing growth of the movement cannot be sustained simply by the conscientious training of leaders. It is dependent on these leaders training others in what is called "just in time training." A primary church leader does not need all the curriculum of what might be taught in seminary to pastor the church; he needs to be equipped for what he needs at the time. If you have ever seen a row of ducklings following the mother duck in a single file you may not have realized they are not all following the mother; each one is following the duck in front of him. By giving leaders the training they need in a way they can pass it on to others immediately as they acquire it, a long educational process that delays effective evangelism and church growth is eliminated. Many missionaries across the world are calling this "T4T" or "training for trainers." In whatever training is being done, the object is not just training the individuals being trained, but training them to train others.

In China, when a new believer is won to the Lord, he is immediately trained and encouraged to win others. As he does, he is then trained how to gather them into a church. As he is being mentored in leading the church, he is training others in the group how to witness and start a church themselves.

CPM STRATEGIES

Our basic purpose is to give all peoples an opportunity to hear, understand, and respond to the gospel. It is necessary for the gospel to be communicated in their own cultural context rather than their having to cross ethnic, language, and geographic barriers. Church-planting movements are the only way the gospel can spread spontaneously and provide all people access to the message of saving faith in Christ. Rapidly multiplying congregations are the only way a massive number of new believers can be discipled and nurtured in their faith. Therefore, it is imperative that our mission strategies facilitate this movement. But how can Southern Baptist churches in the United States be involved in an indigenous strategy that can result in kingdom growth to the ends of the earth?

It is evident that only God can start and precipitate a church-planting movement. It is a spiritual movement that affirms the power of the gospel to change lives and spreads through the fervent witness of new believers. Implementing prescribed methods and following certain steps provide no guarantee a CPM will occur. God, in His providence, chooses to move in His timing in certain places and among certain peoples. But we can learn how to cooperate with God in His divine activity, knowing that He desires for all men to repent and come to the knowledge of the truth. And we can avoid imposing obstacles that inhibit the spontaneous movement of His Spirit.

Several common factors have been identified wherever indigenous churches are multiplying rapidly. One is the evidence of prayer being vital and prominent in the lives of the missionary, the new churches, and their leaders. Prayer is the source of power for evangelistic harvest and subsequent church growth. And often it is discovered that there is a prayer network of churches and partners abroad that have adopted the people group and have been fervently interceding and praying for the people.

Another element is abundant sowing of the gospel, sometimes for years. Saturation of the gospel is always a precursor to church growth. It is presumptuous and a mistake to think that one can implement church-planting methodology without extensive evangelistic witnessing, sometimes for years. Media tools, Bible and literature distribution, verbal proclamation, and personal witness can all be used effectively. The method is not as important as the conviction that God indwells the message and truth of the gospel, and it will draw people to faith in Christ.

There is no exception to scriptural authority in a church-planting movement. In my own earlier years of church planting, as groups of new believers came together and churches were formed, I became frustrated by one aspect of the Great Commission. Jesus instructed us to "teach them all things I have commanded you." New Christians usually had no background whatsoever for understanding anything related to the Bible, the church, and the Christian way of life. I had spent my time introducing the claims of Jesus and cultivating their understanding and acceptance of the plan of salvation. As they came to the point of commitment and obedience in baptism, I began to contemplate what should be the first thing I taught them. What was the most important priority? Then what was the next most important lesson they should learn as new Christians? As I outlined all the essentials that Jesus taught, I began to realize that it would take years to cover these lessons, meeting with each church once a week.

It was in this context that I came to understand that Jesus was saying to teach them obedience. We had already made Bibles available, and they were reading them diligently. The task of making disciples, following baptism, involved teaching them that the Bible was the true, revealed Word of God. They were to read it, study it, meditate upon it, and believe it. They were to obediently follow its instruction and teaching. Churches that rapidly multiply and share their faith do so from conviction regarding the authority of God's Word for all matters of faith and practice.

Another element is intentional church planting. Churches don't just happen. What is done in evangelism and ministry should be done in such a way that enables new believers to be won and gathered into congregations. But then it is contingent on local lay leaders and the churches meeting in facilities that they themselves provide. It is important that missionaries and volunteer groups who work and witness faithfully do so, not for whatever may result from their efforts, but in a way that enables indigenous churches to be planted.

In one restrictive country where a limited number of churches are in existence, the authorities refused to allow any new churches to be built or started. They said, "You Christians will just have to meet in your homes." The historically slow growth of these established churches literally exploded with hundreds of house churches spreading in every village and community. Now everyone is in close proximity to a church, and the informal home setting makes it conducive for unsaved neighbors to attend and hear the gospel.

In one region overseas, the role of the missionary and partners reaching a people group, city, or population segment through potential church-planting movements was outlined as follows:

- **Live Incarnationally**
- **Pray Intensely**
- **Sow Immensely**

- **Harvest Intentionally**
- **Disciple Infectiously**
- **Congregate Immediately**
- **Function Indigenously**
- **Equip Informally**
- **Lead Inconspicuously**
- **Multiply Infinitely**

The size, venue, and functioning of house churches may be similar to cell groups, but churches that rapidly multiply are not a part of a mega-church or centralized ecclesiastical identity. Each one is independent and autonomous. They grow by multiplying and starting other groups from their evangelistic efforts. Unlike many traditional churches that grow to the point of having to provide special facilities and programs, they are not ingrown, but rather focus on starting new congregations. The vitality of a church and necessity of the lay witness are diminished as professional full-time staff assume the responsibilities for evangelism, leadership, and ministry. As a congregation grows, greater attention to its own internal needs tends to take priority over starting new churches and missionary outreach.

One obstacle to church growth is a contextualized ecclesiology, that is, a concept of what a church is in a certain culture. This concept usually contains extraneous and superfluous elements that are inconsistent with the biblical and spiritual nature of a church. In the book of Acts, we see the spontaneous growth of the church that was resulting from a Spirit-indwelt, regenerate covenant community. The believers were, "day by day continuing with one mind in the temple, and breaking bread from house to house . . . praising God, and having favor with all the people. And the Lord was adding to their number day by day those who were being saved" (Acts 2:46–47). Subsequent passages reveal that, "multitudes of men and women were constantly added to their number . . . And every day, in the temple and from house to house, they kept right on teaching and preaching Jesus as the Christ" (Acts 5:14 and 42).

Not only did the number of believers and disciples increase, in Jerusalem thousands of them met daily in houses as they gathered in a visible expression of the fellowship of believers. Their witness was evident—every day new believers were coming to faith in Christ. In Acts 9:31 we are told that the church continued to increase, and in Acts 16:5 that the churches themselves increased in number daily. As the believers dispersed, church-planting movements followed.

Another obstacle to church planting and multiplication growth is seeking to help these churches in a way that actually hurts them spiritually and inhibits their effectiveness. We are in an era of increased involvement in international missions. Partnerships and volunteer projects take many Southern Baptists overseas. Americans are often unprepared for the poverty and economic disparity they find. The compassionate desire to help believers and churches out of our abundance and Western affluence is commendable. But many are blind to the dangers of a valid spiritual ministry degenerating into material assistance that is detrimental to the health and growth of a church. Our mission efforts must result in churches that can exist, grow, and multiply within their own culture and economy without dependence on foreign resources.

Many years of missionary work around the world has taught us it is a mistake to try to accelerate growth through the infusion of financial aid to build churches and support pastors. Well-intended financial assistance too often creates dependence and handicaps the initiative and faith that is essential to growth. It creates a patronizing welfare mentality on the part of local believers. Potential growth often stalls because local people are led to believe that it can't be done unless an overseas benefactor provides the funds.

When that happens, the congregation loses a sense of ownership and ceases to be a responsible and conscientious steward, since others are providing the financial needs of the pastor and church. Jealousy often develops among the pastors and churches who don't receive assistance. They envy those who develop a pipeline of support from the United States through their contacts with volunteers and others. Cooperation between churches diminishes since they no longer have to work together in mutual support, encouragement, and interdependency.

Eventually the support from abroad breeds resentment, especially if the support is not sustained indefinitely. The donor is under the illusion of assisting just until the church can grow to self-support, but that seldom happens. People are deprived of the opportunity to grow in faith, learn to depend on God, and discover that He is sufficient for all their needs. Financial subsidy from abroad also reinforces and propagates a Western model of a church that sees a building and a paid pastor as essential, rather than encouraging a reproducible biblical model of the church as gathered believers responsible for their own leadership and facilities.

The work of missionaries is also often undercut. They seek to witness and minister in a spiritual partnership with local believers that can result in growing and multiplying indigenous churches. They are seen as uncaring when they don't provide the same material and financial aid that volunteers and churches in the States are willing to provide. Often indigenous churches do grow sufficiently to call and support a full-time pastor and build worship facilities, but when they have been self-supporting from the beginning, they know their growth is the result of spiritual vitality.

Church growth can be deterred when others are "hired" to do the work. Multitudes of national church planters are being supported from abroad to start churches, especially where there is a dearth of Western missionaries. To the extent they exercise a catalytic role and engage in strategies to train lay pastors to generate indigenous work, the methodologies are valid. But it is difficult even for national workers to avoid creating dependency when they become the primary leader and depend on support from outside resources rather than the local congregation.

Many prominent mission agencies promote the support of national pastors and evangelists on the basis that they are cheaper than Western missionaries. It is reasoned that they are more effective since they don't have to learn a new language and they can serve in their own culture. As mentioned earlier, the IMB is involved in training more than 120,000 national workers each year; it is the apex of an indigenous church-planting strategy. But these national workers are dependent on local support, not the IMB. Simply being a national evangelist or a cross-cultural Western missionary is no guarantee of effectiveness or success. The key is whether or not one has the anointing of God's Holy Spirit.

The explosive growth of the church in China would never have occurred had dependency on missionary societies continued. The highest rate of church growth is occurring in some of the most impoverished countries of the world. Baptists in Malawi started almost one church for every two already organized in a recent year. Bangladesh reports 7,800 new churches started in the last 10 years; this is a country where the annual per capita income is less than 100 dollars. The growth in Cambodia mentioned earlier occurred in one of the poorest nations in Southeast Asia.

On the other hand, growth proceeds slowly and incrementally where well-meaning supporters from abroad insist on providing the financial aid. Some areas of Latin America exhibit all the conditions for an evangelistic harvest, yet church growth is minimal because of the dependency created by partners from the United States. A few years ago a state convention enthusiastically entered into a partnership with an Eastern European country. As an element of the partnership, every new church-planting effort was funded by churches in America. They met their goal of starting 20 churches in five years—providing salaries for the church planters and pastors and funding for the church buildings. Meanwhile a neighboring country with similar conditions and responsiveness saw more than 200 new churches planted in the same time frame. Churches in the second country are continuing to reproduce since they were never dependent upon foreign subsidy.

I recently visited one of the most impoverished, restricted countries in the world. The average salary is equivalent to nine dollars a month. The wind of the Spirit was blowing with phenomenal numbers of baptisms and church growth. One of the pastors said that he did not suffer because of what he did not have. He testified, "Because we have God, we have everything!"

Many things can be done through overseas partnerships to glorify God and extend His kingdom without creating dependency. There should be no reticence in coming alongside Baptist partners in other countries to demonstrate our love and the compassion of Jesus in ministering to human suffering and providing equipping ministries. Resources can be provided to make Bibles available, to furnish media tools, translation projects, television broadcasts, the *JESUS* film, and printed literature. Theological education—though a primary responsibility of the churches being served—is an area of valid partnership.

But the contribution of overseas partners and mission agencies must always be a spiritual one. A church-planting movement is not contingent on budget or property. When well-intentioned outsiders prop up growth by purchasing and building buildings or subsidizing pastors' salaries, they limit the capacity of the movement to reproduce itself spontaneously and indigenously. We may take pride in helping a local church and seeing it grow, but in doing so we may short-circuit an approach that could have resulted in the whole area being evangelized. We must remember that our mission task is about lostness and reaching the whole world.

Does an emphasis on a strategy focused on indigenous church-planting movements imply other kinds of missions work such as health care, agriculture, social work, and theological education are not important? Does promoting an awareness of the many still Unreached People Groups imply that reaping the harvest on open, evangelized fields is not a valid need? Does changing organizational structures and field strategies to be more relevant for the future mean that previous methodologies were ineffective? Not at all!

Those who have difficulty working with the tensions of dichotomies and change fail to recognize it is not a matter of "either/or" but one of choosing priorities. An unwillingness to focus on strategic priorities may be the greatest contributor to mediocrity. A budget dollar can be spent only once. Personnel can be deployed only one place or another. Choices have to be made if the objective of reaching all peoples and fulfilling the Great Commission is to be accomplished. It is not a matter of choosing between good and bad or what is effective or ineffective; that would be easy. Determining priorities requires a resolve and commitment to what most effectively fulfills one's purpose. Keeping appropriate balance is a necessity and a challenge.

For all peoples to come to faith in Jesus Christ, someone has to take the gospel to the Unreached People Groups who have never heard. While preachers, evangelists, and church planters represent the cutting edge of witness, less than 30 percent of IMB personnel are assigned to those categories of service. Every missionary must be involved in evangelism and the comprehensive task of discipleship, training, and church planting to assure the hoped-for results. For the task to be accomplished, skilled personnel engaged in media, publications, development, medical ministries, and scores of other platforms are responsible for opening doors, touching hearts, and creating an environment for response.

We will always struggle with the tension between dispersion and concentration of missionary personnel. With limited numbers of missionaries, what is an appropriate proportion between those sowing in places where the harvest has not yet emerged and training and partnering with nationals to accelerate the harvest where the gospel has been proclaimed in abundance?

The world is constantly changing. If an organization or strategy does not change, it will only become irrelevant and ineffective. Should one neglect new, emerging opportunities to maintain historic commitments? To what extent should priority be given to relating to established work and seeing immediate results if it means forfeiting the long-range potential in new fields and people groups that are becoming accessible? These choices are not about what is right or wrong but determining an appropriate balance and a commitment to what most effectively reaches the whole world.

Individual missionaries struggle with the tension between mobility and staying in a location indefinitely. Longevity is usually a guarantee of greater results locally, but working with an exit perspective usually results in the more effective training of local believers, relinquishing of leadership, and covering more territory in successive or multiple assignments.

Every generation of missionaries—and each successive era of leadership—at the IMB has been committed to fulfilling God's calling and seizing the current opportunity to reach a lost world through the most effective and relevant strategies. It would be foolish to continue doing things as they have always been done without recognizing the world is changing and each generation is confronted with new opportunities and potential that did not exist previously. It is essential to examine every decision in light of the vision of an evangelized world and what it will take to reach all peoples.

We are stewards of the gospel, called to obedience and commissioned to disciple all peoples. Church-planting movements are accelerating the harvest and providing access to the gospel beyond our missionary witness. We dare not engage in strategies that would deter the movement of God and divert us from the vision of reaching the whole world.

CHAPTER FIVE

COOPERATING IN KINGDOM GROWTH

It is not the responsibility of the International Mission
Board to do missions on behalf of Southern Baptists;
the Great Commission was given to every church, every
believer and every denominational entity. The IMB is to
serve, facilitate, and enable God's people to be
obedient to our Great Commission task.

The comprehensive nature of our mission task and the cooperative ways Southern Baptists work together became apparent during
a temporary assignment to India several years ago. It was 1979, and I
had spent almost 10 years in Indonesia. Located five hours from the
nearest missionary colleague, we had worked alone and in relative isolation throughout those early years on the mission field. I had been
asked to go to India for several months to train national workers and
help missionaries develop a strategy that would result in more effective
church growth. Southern Baptists were rather new to India. Access
became a reality when Jasper McPhail, a cardiovascular surgeon,

responded to God's call to this populous nation in 1963. Other doctors joined him, and a hospital was built in Bangalore in 1968.

For 10 years, the missionary medical staff had hired national evangelists to witness to hospital patients and to follow up their witness throughout the city and in the surrounding villages. When a group of believers emerged within a village or neighborhood, the missionaries requested funds from the International Mission Board to buy land and build a church. Once an evangelist began to pastor one or two of these churches, time and availability for further evangelistic outreach diminished and other evangelists had to be hired.

After a decade of effective ministry in a place of fertile soil and responsive harvest, 21 churches had been started and the annual mission budget was consistently overextended. Yet with this growth came a high level of frustration. The potential for continued growth was promising but resources for buying land, building churches, and supporting national workers was limited.

After arriving in Bangalore, I spent three months accompanying the pastors and evangelists to the villages and learning the culture. Having become accustomed to the restrictions of a Muslim country in Indonesia, I was amazed at the freedom to preach and witness openly in India. It would take months of going to various offices and getting permits to show a film in Indonesia, but in India the teams would walk into a town, set up the equipment, gather a crowd, and show the film without any preliminary hassle. I had never engaged in street preaching previously, but not wanting to be left behind, I jumped right in when someone would say, "Let's start preaching," in the midst of a busy market area! Everywhere we went people seemed eager to hear the gospel.

I learned to be cautious of anyone who readily made a commitment. The plurality of religious beliefs within this Hindu culture allowed them to easily embrace and incorporate Jesus into their pantheon of gods. There were radicals who heckled and sought to disrupt every evangelistic effort. Our workers received their share of persecution, often being threatened, beaten, and stoned. But they were undeterred and persevered. I never got used to the darkness and depravity of those who worshiped idols and were locked into the hopeless bondage of the caste system and the endless cycle of reincarnations, so it was no surprise when we witnessed a phenomenal response to the gospel.

But my greatest burden after seeing the gospel proclaimed and people respond was the evangelists moving on without ever incorporating new believers into a church. I began the training sessions with our missionaries and national co-workers, beginning with a biblical study of the New Testament church. We observed in the book of Acts that as people received the truth of the gospel, the Holy Spirit drew them together into a *koinonia* fellowship to worship and to be discipled. They learned from the teaching of the apostles and reached out to others in witness and ministry. They recognized gifts of the Spirit that God gave to each one within the local body to equip and complete the church, including those with pastoral, teaching, administrative, and evangelistic gifts.

We began to analyze the elements of what Christians in India perceived to be essential to the existence of a church. Permanent facilities, a specific number of baptized members, and a full-time, ordained pastor were among things that were listed. Yet when we compared this to the New Testament model, the group discovered there was no biblical rationale for many of the elements their traditions and perception imposed. As they began to understand the spiritual power of the gospel and the biblical and spiritual nature of the church, the number of congregations began to multiply. There was a liberating effect as churches—and the expanding network of believers—were no longer dependent on evangelists and pastors hired and supported by the mission. Believers shared their faith freely with their extended family and in neighboring villages. As missionaries, evangelists, and hospital staff discipled and trained lay pastors, they in turn passed on the training to others. During the next 10 years, the 21 churches started in the first decade of our work multiplied to more than 400!

Diversity and Platforms

One of the reasons the gospel could be planted and kingdom growth occur in this situation was the amazing synergy that grew out of diverse and comprehensive missionary assignments and the cooperative involvement of Southern Baptists beyond the work of the missionaries themselves. It happened because of a unique synergy of missionaries working with local Baptists, networking with other evangelicals, and implementing creative strategies that allowed the power of God to work in a fruitful way.

For years Southern Baptists had tried to gain entry into India, only to be frozen out. The problem was not government restrictions or religious opposition. The India Christian Council, to whom the government relinquished oversight of Christian missionaries, simply would not grant permission. But due to the expertise and credentials of Dr. McPhail, the opportunity for a medical ministry emerged. Once the door was opened, the ministries and impact of Southern Baptists continued to expand.

God-called physicians joined the team along with nurses and a lab technician. Nutritionists and community health workers initiated programs that reached into far-flung villages and touched an impoverished society at its point of need. Agricultural consultants, university teachers, and student workers expanded the witness. Business consultants brought in micro-enterprises that engendered self-sufficiency and improved the quality of life. All of these, in their distinct and unique ways, contributed to cultivating the hearts of people to be receptive to the Christian message.

Compassion for the people of India and recognition that their experience and training had equipped them for a unique contribution to kingdom growth motivated these missionaries to leave their comfort zones in America in response to God's call. This diverse group of gifted personnel, while carrying out their assignments with integrity, came alongside the multiplying house churches to give encouragement and training.

So it is all over the world. This historical pattern in India is being replicated in countries long restricted to a missionary presence. People with comprehensive skills and professional experience are accepting assignments that are opening doors of opportunity to share the gospel. Local indigenous churches are coming into existence among previously Unreached People Groups because of a diverse team committed to going to the ends of the earth in order to grow the kingdom of God.

There is a mistaken perception that the International Mission Board is interested in appointing and sending out only evangelists and church planters. The reality is that there are scores of personnel requests for a diversity of vocational skills to fill critical niches in mission strategies. In fact, until recent efforts in the Office of Mission Personnel consolidated the lists, there were more than 100 categories of missionary assignment. These included accountants and business managers to handle the support needed by more than 5,000 personnel involved in 184 countries around the world.

Church planters, general evangelists, and seminary teachers are not the only ones needed. There are requests for the full spectrum of health-care workers, including doctors with various specialties, nurses, public health workers, and medical technicians. As people with these skills continue to flow to the field, they are no longer restricted to an institutional mission hospital but are teaching in government medical schools and extending a healing ministry in remote locations that have no Christian witness. Today agriculturists, veterinarians, development workers, media specialists, sports trainers, computer technicians, English teachers—almost every conceivable skill—have a place on the mission field. Many of these are providing a platform for access into restricted countries that do not allow a missionary presence.

A platform is something you stand on. The professional credentials and experience of many being called today allow them as teachers, doctors, businessmen, and social workers to plant their lives in places the gospel could not otherwise be shared. Those early missionaries who responded to the open door in India did not call their assignments a platform, but that is what they were. The medical work and professional skills that justified their entry into the country were the platform that made their presence possible.

Many who use platforms to gain entry and a witness in restricted countries cannot be identified openly as missionaries nor can they be linked with the International Mission Board. It would not only jeopardize their continuing presence, causing them to forfeit their witness and ministry, but, in some cases, it could endanger the lives of local believers. Yet these personnel provide a vital service in meeting the needs of the community—a benefit desired by officials in developing nations. They go to fulfill their assignment with integrity. Their presence is a "value-added" service, legitimized by work permits granted by the government.

Almost every country opens its doors to some type of foreign residents. The issue is discovering skills that are needed and what type of foreign individual is acceptable. Open preaching and witnessing may be prohibited, but one's presence becomes an incarnational witness of living out one's faith before friends and neighbors. Those relationships invariably lead to an opportunity to give an explanation and verbal witness of what one believes. The Holy Spirit that indwells the message of the gospel begins to draw the hearts of others to embrace faith in Jesus Christ. Opportunities for nurturing new believers in their faith and understanding the Bible emerge. Cultivating groups of "inquirers" to come together for mutual strength and encouragement leads to churches being planted. And a nucleus of witness is established in places where the gospel has not been known.

Some would challenge the ethics of a covert witness, saying that missionaries should go only where they are welcomed and can witness openly and freely. Such an attitude expresses a shallow level of obedience to our Lord, who told us to disciple all nations. It belittles the lostness of people without access to the gospel and disregards our responsibility to "preach the gospel to all creation" (Mark 16:15). It also fails to recognize the sense in which every Christian is to be a missionary. Certainly there are those called to a cross-cultural missionary role, but must that be restricted to preachers and evangelists? If we are all to be witnesses where we live within our community and among our co-workers and those with whom we interact as we shop and handle routine business, shouldn't we do that overseas as well? Is it inappropriate to intentionally seek such an opportunity in places that do not have a church on every corner proclaiming the gospel? Our presence, welcomed as a teacher or business consultant, may be the only chance someone has to hear of Jesus.

Governments that are paranoid about missionaries proselytizing their people still need computer engineers, medical workers, and English teachers from abroad. Shouldn't Christians be willing to respond to those requests? If Christians are allowed to gain entry to restricted nations in professional roles, should not the IMB facilitate qualified individuals filling these needs?

The early disciples were sent into a hostile environment where their witness was not welcomed by the local religious authorities or by the Roman political regime. They were threatened, arrested, and some eventually martyred because of their faithfulness and persistence in sharing the gospel. Yet when they were ordered not to speak or teach in the name of Jesus—just as many missionary personnel serving in the Muslim world are today—they replied, "We must obey God rather than men" (Acts 5:29). Peter had said on an earlier occasion, "we cannot stop speaking about what we have seen and heard" (Acts 4:20).

When one has had the privilege of knowing Jesus in a life-changing experience of salvation, there should be a compulsion to do whatever it takes to share Him with others. There should be a willingness to endure ridicule, to risk repercussions and even danger so that others would have the opportunity of knowing Jesus. In His final exhortation to His followers, Jesus expressed the passion and urgency of extending the kingdom to the ends of the earth. He did not say to go and make disciples wherever it is safe and legal to do so. He did not qualify His instructions to witness to the ends of the earth on where you are welcome to do so. There were no contingency clauses; the mandate was all nations and all peoples, regardless!

An example of this approach is the nation of Cambodia. In the early 1990s, this beautiful little country in Indochina was still under communist rule and missionary presence was restricted. But following the reign of Pol Pot and the Khmer Rouge—and the tragic genocide in which millions were killed or displaced—the country was destitute and in need of social help and rehabilitation. Several social workers were enlisted to risk going into this foreboding environment with a registered, non-government humanitarian agency. They provided medical care, improved sanitation, and helped create better working conditions in the factories. Others joined the team who were qualified to install water purification equipment, design systems for sewage disposal, rebuild schools, and contribute to educational programs. They carried out their assignments professionally and won the favor of government and community officials.

Within two years, 24 house churches had emerged in the capital city of Phnom Penh. Two years later a nationwide Baptist convention was formed with 43 organized churches. Five years later there were more than 200 Baptist churches. This didn't happen through missionary church planters blitzing the country in an open witness, but through national believers sharing their faith. They were trained and encouraged by missionaries whose diversity of skills and assignments enabled them to have access to the country. They seized the opportunity for an incarnational presence and witness by providing a value-added service to a country and people in need.

In another part of Asia, an agricultural missionary felt led to use his skills to help the people of Orissa, considered to be the most impoverished state in all of India. He was able to get a visa through an arrangement to teach at an agricultural university. With national colleagues at the university, he set up agricultural training centers among the Kui tribal group in the remote Khond Hills. The program proved to be effective, and the training was valued and appreciated. Locally trained evangelists followed up the agricultural training in the villages. Eventually, many of the participants in the training became itinerant, lay evangelists after being exposed to the gospel. As more and more people responded and began to share their faith, the missionary said he couldn't really tell if they were farmers doing evangelism or evangelists supporting themselves by farming!

Later he and an IMB media consultant assigned to Asia collaborated in the production of a daily, 15-minute radio program in the Kui language. It was the only broadcast in the language of these tribal people. News quickly spread through the villages that they could tune in at a certain time and frequency and hear the radio in their own heart language. Listener groups formed spontaneously all over the Khond Hills. People would stop what they were doing to listen to this program, which featured agricultural and community development information, and then segued into sharing the gospel. The people sat around and discussed what they had heard, and reports grew of many coming to faith in Christ. The local evangelists could not keep up with the churches being started and the requests from more distant villages to come and teach them how to become followers of Christ.

As the work grew, itinerant missionaries who could not live in India came regularly for short periods to assist with training. One year after the broadcast was begun, 80 new churches had been started and more than 5,000 Kui believers were baptized. The movement now reports 2,249 churches, and evangelistic efforts by the Kui have spread to several neighboring tribes. The Lord used many factors to bring about such a harvest, but the synergy of a lone agriculturist who was willing to go to a remote and isolated assignment, a missionary devoted to using media, and some itinerant missionaries willing to leave their assignment in another country all converged to allow God to work.

STRATEGIC FOCUS AND COORDINATION

Kingdom advance in India and around the world is not simply the work of American missionaries. One person on the ground and several others assisting from distant locations could not produce more than 2,000 churches in the Khond Hills. Twenty-one churches could not multiply to more than 400 in South India because of some medical workers, or a nationwide Baptist convention formed in Cambodia because of some social work platforms. It happened because of a methodology that focused on training new believers and allowed the power of the gospel to be unleashed. A pyramiding program of discipleship was initiated that spread beyond the reach of the missionary to produce growing and multiplying churches. God was able to bless these efforts because they entailed strategies and methods that provided a context for Him to work in a way that was consistent with biblical models.

"Strategy" is a military term that means a plan or technique for accomplishing an objective. It implies there is an enemy or impediment to the desired objective. In the task of advancing God's kingdom and claiming the peoples of the world for Jesus Christ, it definitely entails spiritual warfare against the principalities and powers of darkness. If any program or endeavor demands wisdom and planning for how to do the job, it is the task of missions. It is inexcusable to approach such an awesome task in a passive or haphazard way. It is unacceptable to simply do what we can and be satisfied with whatever may result.

It is easy to be diverted by the urgency of the moment or circumstances that take our vision off the overall objective. Many allow presence itself and secondary ministries to become the main focus rather than seeing them as a means to an end. Others embrace a methodology that strengthens one local church and wins a few converts for what could have initiated a movement toward Christ among a whole people group or population segment. The IMB defines its basic strategy—how it accomplishes its task—as sending and supporting missionaries to proclaim the gospel in a way that results in multiplying indigenous Baptist churches. This is discussed more thoroughly in chapters 4 and 6.

A strategic focus keeps us from simply doing more of what we have already been doing in more places without results. It keeps us from dissipating resources on secondary ministries and projects that do not lead to our main objective of kingdom growth among all peoples. It keeps us from isolating any one aspect of our task to the neglect of others. Someone has said, "If you don't know where you are going, any road will do." However, if one knows where he wants to go, it is important to take the right road. We know where we want to go, so we must not take roads that lead elsewhere.

Strategic planning identifies the road to take, and strategy determines the use of budget resources and missionary deployment, not vice versa. Those who determine strategy must be closest to the action; those who are responsible for implementing strategies must have ownership for formulating them. The International Mission Board does not have a common global strategy. The world is too diverse for a common approach. We have a focused purpose that all peoples would know Christ. We have a unified vision to bring all peoples to saving faith in Jesus Christ and agreement that indigenous church-planting movements is the only way the gospel will be made accessible to all peoples. But cultures and languages are different. Responsiveness is varied. The history and maturity of Baptist partners are diverse all over the world. Those in the best position to determine the strategy—the *how to*—in initiating and facilitating local church-planting movements are the missionaries who have planted their lives, learned the language, and are relating to national partners among the peoples to be reached.

For this reason, field missionaries are now organized in localized teams, each one focused on a specific people group or segment of the population. Other support teams provide business management serv-ices for those in a given country or area. In most instances, whole countries are too large and complex to represent a common approach or strategy. When missionaries were organized according to the country in which they resided, some areas received all the attention and resources while other vast areas and peoples were neglected. The large mission structures required an inordinate amount of time and resources just to administer the needs and affairs of the missionaries themselves. In contrast, mission teams are accountable to one another and are focused on a shared goal and objective, supporting one another and applying their diversity of gifts and skills to a common task.

Most teams include a strategy coordinator. This is a missionary who takes responsibility for developing and implementing a strategy for a church-planting movement among a specific target group or area. This role is not as critical where churches have been planted and there are Christians who can assume the continuing responsibility of reaching and evangelizing their people. The strategy coordinator, along with others on the team, engages the people group through direct relationship building, witness, and discipleship. He serves as the team leader, facilitating the involvement and use of each team member's gifts along with other Great Commission partners.

The strategy coordinator is responsible for seeing that a prayer network is developed that guides in the advocacy for the people group among churches in our Southern Baptist constituency. He networks with other mission agencies and organizations to multiply and accelerate engagement among the people group. He is usually innovative and visionary, modeling the training of national believers and leaders, and keeping the team in a catalytic role lest dependency be created. Much of the global advance of the IMB in engaging new people groups is contingent on more missionaries who are gifted and willing to serve as strategy coordinators. When there is cooperation among those with diverse gifts and skills in a focused indigenous strategy, the potential of reaching the whole world is enhanced.

RESPONDING TO SUFFERING AND HUMAN NEED

World events and natural disasters often open areas previously closed or resistant to the gospel. Responding to tragedies and the chronic suffering of people allows the love of God to be demonstrated through compassionate ministries. It is too soon to know what impact ministries following the tsunami of December 2004 will have in the eight Asian nations affected. Southern Baptists contributed nearly 16.5 million dollars to help the people of that region rebuild their lives; relationships built through the response of missionaries and volunteer teams will have an impact in advancing the gospel. As hundreds of volunteers worked to dig graves, transport bodies, supply health care, distribute food, provide counseling, and help in resettlement camps, they reflected an incarnational witness in some of the most resistant and closed areas of the world.

In the 1970s Southern Baptists established a World Hunger Offering in response to the famine in Ethiopia. These offerings and relief efforts in response to floods, earthquakes, droughts, and other disasters have contributed significantly to kingdom growth. When Hurricane Mitch roared across Honduras in October 1998, Southern Baptists once again responded. They filled 80 40-foot shipping containers with more than 2 million pounds of food, blankets and clothing. Medical workers came to treat the survivors. More than 2,000 volunteers worked through the IMB to build 600 cinder-block houses across the ravaged country.

"In dealing with the physical needs of the people, we were also able to deal with their spiritual needs," said Max Furr, an IMB missionary who was disaster response coordinator for the IMB's relief efforts at the time. "We encountered an openness for the gospel never before seen here in Honduras," reported Furr. While countrywide thousands lost their lives, thousands more found eternal life. The relief efforts resulted in 78 new Baptist churches across the country. In one of the hardest hit areas, 800 decisions for Christ were recorded.

But natural disasters are not the only situations that create sudden, unique opportunities. Some are precipitated by events that develop more slowly. Population pressure in developing nations forces people to farm land once considered unsuitable for agriculture. Hillsides and mountainsides are stripped of trees and natural cover to plant crops. Because of the steep slopes, it is not long before the topsoil erodes, sending silt into rivers and streams, resulting in a barren, unproductive landscape. Fish disappear from the waters, wildlife that once populated the area vanish, productivity decreases, and people go hungry.

Harold Watson, IMB missionary to the Philippines, began addressing this problem in 1971. He looked for a way to help people feed themselves while extending the gospel. From the start, he looked for a way to integrate agriculture into a program that encouraged church growth. He persuaded the IMB to buy a small parcel of barren land on the island of Mindanao and open a research and demonstration farm called the Rural Life Center. On it he developed a program called SALT (Sloping Agricultural Land Technology). It uses appropriate technology to help hungry upland farmers stop soil erosion and grow more food.

Farmers use a simple A-frame device to measure the slope of a hillside and determine where to plant fast-growing trees. The trees are planted inches apart in a number of rows spaced across a hillside. They immediately begin to replenish the soil with nitrogen. The trees are trimmed back 10 times a year to form hedgerows. Hillside erosion fills in the gaps between the hedgerows and forms flat, natural terraces of rich, productive soil that can be farmed. It is simple technology that can easily be understood and replicated. Through the years a number of programs were developed to train people in these techniques. All of the programs combine agricultural training with Bible training. "Our ambition," said Watson, "was not only to help someone grow more corn. Our vision from the beginning was to make a better farmer a better Christian." A program to accomplish this objective is called BOOST (Baptists Out of School Training).

Another program, called TEACH (Tribal Evangelism, Agriculture, Church, and Healthcare), has spread the influence and witness of the Rural Life Center into remote areas. Within five years of beginning these programs, 20 churches formed in the area around the center. Since then, more than 130 have been started and about 30 percent of the 1,700 Baptist churches on Mindanao are now led by graduates of the Rural Life Center training programs. Watson has since retired, but others continue the programs, and these kinds of ministries have been replicated all over the world. The techniques Watson pioneered are now used across Asia and beyond, in places like Indonesia, Vietnam, Mexico, India, and Nepal.

Medical work, humanitarian efforts, agricultural projects, and educational ministries can be carried out as an end in themselves. But missionaries who are involved in such enterprises are motivated by God's call to share more than agricultural techniques or relief with those who are suffering. They go because of a desire greater than merely addressing humanitarian needs. Something more than healing sick bodies, improving the quality of life, and advancing the educational level in developing countries compels them to give of their lives. They do what they do so that all peoples will have an opportunity to know Jesus and the kingdom of God can be advanced to the ends of the earth.

All missionaries are not full-time church planters. But the desire of every missionary is to see believers come to faith, form into local, indigenous churches, and be trained to continue a kingdom witness. Kingdom growth has a narrow and singular objective, yet it involves comprehensive strategies and diverse gifts for evangelizing the lost, discipling believers, planting and developing churches, training leaders, and ministering to people in need.

A missionary assigned to community development in West Africa recently put this in perspective. With a doctorate in public health, he is well-qualified. He told of how entire villages had been rehabilitated by their programs, which included providing pure drinking water, improving sanitation, and educating the people regarding nutrition and health. After recounting statistics and describing the community impact he had seen, he began to weep. Sobbing, he said, "We have accomplished all our objectives this term, but I have been a failure." After gaining his composure he continued, ". . . because none of these people have trusted in Christ, and healthy in hell doesn't count for much." He expressed the driving passion behind every missionary, regardless of the role. Why would we help them in meeting needs for this life and neglect to prepare them for eternity?

Cooperative Support

Focused strategies, comprehensive methods, diverse skills, and creative platforms of a multitude of missionaries could not extend God's kingdom to the ends of the earth without the cooperative support and involvement of God's people. No one is exempt from the Great Commission mandate of our Lord. The exciting advance of God's kingdom is occurring because Southern Baptists are discovering channels for personalized involvement in the task. That involvement is more than just meeting the responsibility to support the work of missionaries; it includes responding to an increasing number of short-term volunteer opportunities. Churches are needed to come alongside the overseas missionary in partnerships that reinforce their strategies, supplement their efforts, and multiply their witness.

The SBC was formed in 1845 to consolidate the efforts of many independent, regional mission societies then in existence. It sought to create cooperation through a unified Domestic Mission Board and the Foreign Mission Board. W. B. Johnson—one of the founding leaders of the Southern Baptist Convention—urged the churches to send messengers to the initial organizational convention in Augusta, Georgia, and for these independent societies to convene, "for the purpose of organizing a practical plan on which the energies of the whole Baptist denomination may be elicited, combined and directed in one sacred effort for sending the word of life to idolatrous lands."[1]

Our visionary founders realized, even then, that churches could do more together than they could separately through isolated and fragmented efforts. Because Baptists believe in and practice the priesthood of every believer and the autonomy of each local church, voluntary cooperation is all that links our churches together as a denomination. While we share common doctrines and beliefs, much diversity exists in styles of worship and local ministries. No ecclesiastical authority compels us to work together to fulfill the Great Commission. Our churches do so because they have a common commitment to the Lordship of Jesus Christ. The average Southern Baptist church has fewer than 300 resident members. Many churches, even those that are much larger, struggle to support their staff and respond to the challenge of local ministries. Few would be able on their own to send and support missionaries to proclaim the gospel to foreign lands and pioneer areas of our own country. But through cooperation, more than 10,000 God-called missionaries are able to serve through the North American and International Mission Boards today.

In 2003 international missionaries were involved in starting 21,028 new churches, and 607,132 new believers were baptized around the world. Pastors, church leaders, and students numbering 22,931 received training in residential seminaries and Bible schools. Another 110,356 participated in programs of extension training on the mission field. Books and tracts were published in multiple languages. Millions heard the good news of salvation through television, films, and radio broadcasts. Multitudes received aid and ministry in the aftermath of floods, droughts, earthquakes, and other disasters. Millions received treatment in mission hospitals and clinics. Kingdom growth is occurring among new people groups being touched by the gospel for the first time. All this is happening because of collective efforts to fulfill the mandate of our Lord. Collective efforts, far beyond what any one church could do alone, are enabling us to reach a lost world to the ends of the earth.

Years ago Southern Baptists abandoned a societal approach in which each institution and ministry competed for direct funding and support. In 1925, The Cooperative Program was established to enable each church to voluntarily allocate a percentage of its undesignated receipts to the work of the denomination. Today, those combined gifts provide the basic resources to support the local state convention, six seminaries, other denominational ministries and services, and our mission efforts throughout North America and around the world. The annual Lottie Moon Christmas Offering® for International Missions allows churches to combine additional resources to send and support missionaries. Not one of them has to personally solicit and raise support before fulfilling God's call. Since the founding of the Southern Baptist Convention, more than 18,000 missionaries have been sent across the globe to extend the kingdom of God, assured that Southern Baptist churches would provide their support.

I recently read a report from a well-known missions agency that indicated they had had more than 700 applicants for missionary service the previous year. Of that number, 240 had been approved and completed training, but eventually only 74 made it to the field. The rest were unable to raise sufficient support. Another organization reported a 30 percent attrition rate because their missionaries could not sustain their support once they got to the field. Some have criticized our system of guaranteed support because it is not "faith-based." But I can assure you that it takes a great deal of faith to send out more than 5,000 missionaries and then trust God to move in the hearts of Southern Baptists to give a one-time annual offering of more than 100 million dollars and support a yearly budget of more than a quarter of a billion dollars!

Each year Southern Baptists increase their gifts to the Cooperative Program and annual missions offerings. Yet the increases are minuscule relative to the challenge of kingdom growth and what is needed to reach a lost world. In 2003, international missionary appointments were deferred for the first time since the years of the Great Depression of the 1930s because the number of candidates responding to God's call exceeded the resources being provided by the churches. In each of the two previous years more than a thousand new missionaries were approved and sent to the field. The numbers of those being called are not coincidental. God is opening more doors of witness than ever before and is accelerating a global harvest.

How will we give account to the Lord of the harvest for retaining more and more of our financial resources for our local ministries while ignoring the responsibility to reach the ends of the earth? Not long ago the average Southern Baptist church gave more than 10 percent of their undesignated offerings to the Cooperative Program. Commendably, some continue to give as much as 20 percent and 30 percent to the work of the kingdom beyond their local church budget. However, the average allocation has now dropped below 7 percent. That means that churches retain 93 percent of budget receipts for their own needs. Of the portion that is passed on to the work of the denomination, an average of 64 percent is used by the state convention. That leaves 36 percent for the larger Southern Baptist Convention, half of which comes to the International Mission Board. Starting with that 7 percent allocation from the average church, that calculates to a startling conclusion: a little more than 1 percent of the undesignated receipts of 43,000 churches is given to reach the world beyond our borders.

When all receipts are taken into consideration, including mission offerings, building funds, and other special gifts, Southern Baptist churches reported receiving 9.6 billion dollars in their offering plates in 2003 alone. Of that amount, less than 2.5 percent was channeled to the International Mission Board to evangelize 6 billion lost people around the world. It is not a problem of the economy; God has prospered and blessed Southern Baptists. He is calling us to cooperate to provide missionary support and underwrite the ministries that will take the gospel to all peoples. The Cooperative Program is not an end in itself. It is the means through which every church can have a part in kingdom growth in their state, throughout North America and to the ends of the earth. The challenge is to bring our hearts into conformity with God's purpose and priority and to share His passion for reaching our world.

Volunteers and Personalized Involvement

While record numbers of missionaries are being sent out, Southern Baptists still have just one missionary unit—family or single person— for every 1.6 million people, and not all of them are proportionately deployed to get the gospel to all peoples. We would have to double the number of missionaries just to have one person assigned to every Unreached People Group, some of which number in the millions. Fulfillment of the Great Commission is an auspicious task, unlikely of success if we think it will be done only by an elite cadre of professional, full-time missionaries. The thousands of volunteers who are joining the effort enhance the potential of our witness around the world.

My first experience with short-term volunteers came during my temporary assignment to India years ago. Frequently medical volunteers came to the hospital, contributing their services and training staff. In the evenings they often went to the village churches and found abundant opportunities for an evangelistic witness. They found giving encouragement to the lay pastors to be a gratifying experience. About two years into the emerging church-growth movement, one of the American physicians suggested bringing a group of volunteers to concentrate on evangelistic outreach. We readily agreed that the climate was good for such a project; when he asked how many should be enlisted, we replied, "As many as you can get to come," expecting a group of 12 to 15 people. We were startled to receive news that 55 Americans would be coming.

The Bangalore airport was a circus as the planeload of Americans disembarked. Each person was welcomed with a lei and a friendly *wei* of folded hands in respectful greeting. There was mass confusion getting the luggage and jet-lagged travelers through the crowd of clamoring coolies and beggars and onto buses. After a day of rest and orientation, the group was to be dispersed in pairs with a national counterpart and translator to saturate a neighborhood or village with door-to-door witnessing. Some would share their testimony in public places, and the day would culminate in an evangelistic service at a church or the home of a sympathetic Christian or inquirer in the evening.

There was the full spectrum of Southern Baptists from teen-agers to the senior adults; most had never been overseas before. The 30 hours of travel, including hours in transit lounges in Amsterdam and Delhi, was an abrupt challenge to their Southern provincialism! Several were put on the train to Madras and another group on the plane to Bombay to "share the blessings of their ministry" with fledg-ling churches there. Reminders regarding cultural sensitivities and an absolute prohibition against eating any food on the streets and in homes were a part of each day's briefing. They left the hotel with bottles of water and peanut butter crackers and candy bars to sustain them until their return for a late dinner in the evening. Miraculously only six succumbed to "Delhi belly" after admitting to drinking the sweet, syrupy tea offered as a gesture of hospitality in each home.

All the volunteers had written their personal testimonies, which had been reproduced with the translation on the backside of the paper, to assist the translators and to leave along with some gospel tracts with those they talked to. There were only six pastors in the group, so there was massive panic when each pair of volunteers was told to decide which one would "preach" each night. A telephone lineman expressed the feelings of others in saying he had never preached, didn't have any sermons, and didn't know how. Not until they gathered in the little house groups did the image of an American pulpit vanish, and they recognized the validity of the exhortation to tell a Bible story about Jesus and share the plan of salvation. The telephone lineman was ecstatic as he came into the hotel the first night, reporting that 10 people had prayed to receive Christ in the worship service he had led. At the end of the week more than 2,000 professions of faith were recorded, all in the context of neighborhoods where follow up could be done, and potential churches were started in 18 locations.

Missionaries realized years ago that their witness could be vastly multiplied by teams of short-term volunteers. They could not begin to give attention to all the local Baptist churches on the mission field, but a program linking stateside churches with those overseas proved to provide encouragement and blessings to both. Volunteer teams come for evangelistic emphases; paired with local church members, they witness in the community and lead training on stewardship, discipleship, and many other programs.

As state conventions assumed coordination of prolonged state-to-national partnerships, enlisting volunteers and providing orientation, the numbers of volunteers escalated to more than 30,000 in 2004. Whereas volunteer teams include many pastors and church staff, they are primarily laymen and women who take vacation time and raise their own support for travel and expenses to share the gospel and meet needs on the mission field overseas.

Their impact is as varied as it is valuable. The training of lay pastors that helped precipitate the church-growth movement in Bangalore and Orissa in India, and in Cambodia, was by teams of volunteers who supplemented what the limited number of missionaries on the field were able to do. Whenever natural disaster strikes, Southern Baptist volunteers have been able to respond effectively anywhere in the world. State disaster relief coordinators can mobilize volunteer teams in a moment's notice. Choirs, athletic teams, medical teams, and a variety of other specialized projects provide channels for any-one to share a witness overseas. Tolerating jet lag and strange foods are worth it to share Christ with people who would not otherwise hear. Psalm 110:3 says, "Thy people will volunteer freely in the day of Thy power." God is demonstrating His power all over the world and His people are saying, "I'm available; I'll go and do what I can." And the kingdom continues to grow.

Not only is there a growing interest in occasional participation through short-term mission trips, but churches are becoming more and more interested in direct, ongoing involvement in mission strategies. They are beginning to recognize that God did not call them just to reach their cities and local communities, but each church can have a role in kingdom growth and fulfilling the Great Commission.

In a paradigm shift to partnerships and personalized relationships, the International Mission Board is seeking to provide opportunities for churches to be directly involved in overseas strategies and have ownership of reaching specific population segments. Through years of volunteer involvement, many churches have developed their own independent missions programs in various parts of the world. They have built relationships with national Baptist leaders and discovered they did not need the International Mission Board to provide contacts, arrange projects, and help them make travel arrangements. Unfortunately, independent involvement overseas, without consultation with missionaries on the field, usually becomes narrowly focused and diminishes the potential for strategic impact.

It is a mark of our contemporary society that people and organizations, including churches, are no longer interested in a "middle man" being a mediator between them and the action. They are not interested in having to "jump through bureaucratic hoops" in order to do missions. Churches are willing to cooperate with others but they want a face on missions. They are willing to give generously but they want to be involved with what they are supporting. They want personal relationships with "their" missionaries.

Rather than seeing this as infringing on the programs and strategies of the IMB, it is seen as an asset that radically multiplies the potential for kingdom growth. Missionaries are encouraged to take initiative in asking churches to adopt them as their personal missionaries. These may be churches where they were members or served on the staff, where they grew up or where their parents are members, or it may be a random relationship. Although the gifts and offerings of the church to the Cooperative Program and Lottie Moon Christmas Offering® go to support more than 5,000 international missionaries, they have personalized these channels of support. They know their gifts are helping to meet the needs of "their" missionary.

Churches are adopting other missionaries who have been in their church on stateside assignment or are related to the church's involvement overseas. The missionaries are accountable to communicate and report back to their churches so that churches can stay abreast of what God is doing in distant lands. This personalized relationship makes the prayer ministry of the church more relevant as they respond to specific needs. One missionary organized a personal team of 15 to 20 people in the church he had left to serve as a supportive liaison between his family and the church. They were charged with maintaining contact and ministering to the needs of the missionary family. One was responsible to nurture their prayer network, another to minister to the children by sending toys and gifts occasionally. They checked on the aging parents of the missionaries, arranged for a power of attorney, assisted in storing belongings left behind, and were available to help if something had to be purchased and shipped from the States. This church was not praying for God to bless a nameless and faceless missionary. They felt personally involved in their support and felt with pride that they had a share in the results of their ministry.

Many churches begin personalized involvement in kingdom growth by adopting people groups in a "PRAYERPlus" partnership—praying for the people plus a commitment to do whatever God leads them to do. Other churches are moving beyond partnership with missionary teams to accept the challenge of adopting an Unreached People Group where no missionary is available to be assigned. At this point, the IMB is giving priority to reaching people groups with a population of 100,000 or more in its global strategies. Most of the still Unreached People Groups are "micro-peoples" with populations far less than that. They generally are located in remote mountain districts, untouched by the gospel.

The South America region launched a strategy called REAP (Rapid Entry Advance Plan). They train churches to access the sparsely populated indigenous tribes scattered throughout mountain valleys of the Andes with no gospel witness in their heart language. With the assistance of national Christians who are bilingual, these churches actually function as the strategy coordinators for their people groups. A church in Georgia with 350 members adopted the Corongo Quechua people in Peru. Within two years they had seen 150 people come to faith in

Christ. A church in Mississippi adopted the Yagua people. Others in South Carolina are working with the Ocros and the Chimborazo, and have seen the first church planted. Some of these partner churches were already involved in Peru. They typically went each year to established churches for a week of evangelistic services and backyard Bible clubs. Now they are evangelizing people groups that would not have been reached for years, if ever, if they had needed to wait for a missionary to be assigned.

A Missouri church that averages 550 in Sunday worship has established continuing partnerships in 12 countries. They are training house-church leaders in China, sending several teams a year to Romania and Brazil, and continuing to look for new opportunities to be involved where God is at work. A Florida church focused on a remote area of Brazil beyond the reach of a missionary or national church seven years ago. Last year this continuing personalized involvement resulted in 7,000 professions of faith and 11 new churches. A Texas church, wanting to go to "the edge," has become involved in Vietnam and Afghanistan and has been openly welcomed by officials in those countries because of the ministries they provide!

God's kingdom will continue to grow as we work together in a partnership of missionaries, volunteers and churches cooperating in focused strategies to bring all the peoples of the world to saving faith in Jesus Christ.

1. John T. Christian, *A History of the Baptists Volume 2,* chapter vi, "The Savannah Baptist Society for Foreign Missions," www.pbministries.org/History/John%20T.%20Christian/vol2/history2_part3_06.htm.

CHAPTER SIX

GOING: THE MASTER'S MANDATE FOR KINGDOM GROWTH

IMB BASIC STRATEGY:

Send and support gifted, God-called missionaries who, with mutual respect, accountability and cooperation, carry out the Great Commission in an incarnational witness.

It is not unusual for someone to ask about my own call to missions. Often missionaries give testimonies regarding their call and how they knew with absolute conviction that God had called them to a cross-cultural ministry overseas. To be willing to live in a foreign country without the amenities one is used to in America, and to be separated from family and friends for an extended period of time is not something one would simply choose to do. Most people would acknowledge that there would have to be a divinely implanted sense of God's purpose—and a commitment to be obedient to His will—to motivate someone to go to distant lands, face the challenge of learning a new language, and embrace the apparent sacrifices that accompany a missionary lifestyle.

I can think of many experiences through which God spoke to me and seemed to say that overseas missions was His purpose for me. I was often stirred as I heard missionaries speak in church and could picture myself living in exotic places such as they described. Participating in local mission projects while in college and going on mission trips to impact needy places away from the comforts and familiarity of my own community were gratifying and fulfilling experiences. I could easily picture giving my life to this sort of activity. Had my conviction regarding God's call not already been solid, a summer mission assignment in the Philippines would have readily confirmed it beyond all doubt.

When I try to put my finger on that specific moment of God's call, I think back over these many experiences and inspiring moments at a youth retreat or revival when a commitment or rededication was made. There was a lingering impression that it had something to do with missions. But invariably, as I reflect back over my pilgrimage of discerning and following God's will, I find myself all the way back to my salvation experience as a 10-year-old boy.

I had been raised in church and knew all the Bible stories. I understood why Jesus died on the cross. I had won awards for Scripture memory and could explain the plan of salvation. Many of my friends had made professions of faith at that age and would ask me, "When are you going to join the church?" or, "When are you going to be baptized?" I knew it was something that I needed to do and did not doubt that I would eventually make a decision trusting Christ as my personal Savior. But there never was a compulsion to respond to the invitation and make that public profession of faith until Billy Graham came to Jackson, Mississippi, for a crusade that summer.

Our church was very involved in the crusade, and my family attended faithfully. One night as Dr. Graham spoke and simply explained the gospel in his inimitable style, I realized that I was a sinner separated from God. In that moment all that I had learned and knew about Jesus came into focus. I understood that He died for my sins. I whispered to my father during the invitation that I had prayed the prayer Dr. Graham had led at the conclusion of his message and that

I wanted to respond to the invitation. I felt so happy because I knew that I had entered into a personal relationship with God that was secure for all eternity. I felt such peace and joy as I walked down those stadium steps and across the football field, hand-in-hand with my father. I can remember thinking, "I wish everyone in the world could know Jesus."

I really believe that in my salvation experience God planted the seeds of a call to missions. It was a desire that everyone in the world could also have the experience of knowing Jesus and being made right with God. I have come to believe that is an attitude every born again believer should have. Entering into a personal relationship with Jesus as Savior and Lord should carry with it, not only a desire, but a sense of responsibility to share Christ with others, even the whole world.

A couple of years later I did receive a distinct impression that God was calling me to be a missionary. It was not in church, but in a middle school geography class. I had been nurtured as a new Christian to understand that God had a unique plan and purpose for my life. Already I had begun to pray that He would reveal His will for my life, that I might know what He wanted me to do and focus my education and preparation on it. Of course that was contingent on my willingness to be obedient and follow His direction. But to the best of my understanding, I felt that I had come to an open commitment and surrender to whatever He revealed.

We were studying Asia in that geography class, and I was impressed by the massive population in that part of the world. We learned of their adherence to the teachings of Confucius, of their Buddhist and Taoist beliefs, and the fact that millions, at the time, were being drawn into the atheistic tenets of communism. I realized that literally tens of millions of people in that part of the world were living a lifetime, dying and going to hell, not because they had rejected Jesus Christ, but because they had never heard of Him.

Being a somewhat missions-minded church kid, the thought occurred to me, "Why don't more missionaries go and tell these people about Jesus?" It was as if God immediately reflected that thought back into my own heart, that I had the potential of being one who could go and share the gospel in places where people did not have an opportunity to hear. I never got away from that impression. As my life became one of following as God led, He continued to confirm that overseas missions was, indeed, the direction He was leading.

The way God calls is as diverse as the personalities and backgrounds of the missionaries who respond. The call of many is nurtured from childhood through missions education organizations like Girls in Action and Royal Ambassadors. My own interest in our Sunday afternoon Royal Ambassador chapter was more on playing touch football and the weekly treat that followed at the neighborhood ice cream parlor than on missions. But the constant exposure to programs on remote parts of the world, the excitement of receiving exotic stamps from missionaries, and a growing comprehension of the meaning of the Great Commission left their marks.

I grew up in a church from which a number of missionaries had gone out, and their furlough testimonies left a deep impression. It was also a college church in which I observed students consistently making decisions of commitment to mission service. Many get away from these early divine impressions and are diverted from what they once heard as a call. But for me, as it is for others, the focus was strengthened in a pilgrimage that eventually led to the mission field.

Today, opportunities to participate in short-term volunteer mission trips are being used by God to call many into full-time missions. With more than 25,000 Southern Baptists going on overseas mission trips every year, God is using their experiences to impress upon many of them the potential in their lives of touching a lost world. Exposed to the lostness of a world without Christ, seeing firsthand how God is working through the power of the gospel—and through ordinary people who offer Him their lives—volunteers are returning home with hearts that are open to God's call. As one businessman who sold his home and business and contacted the International Mission Board said, "It is hard to come back home, settle into your comfort zone, enjoy the affluence of an American lifestyle and continue to pursue wealth and the American dream when you have seen a world dying without Christ and know you could do something about it."

A new missionary going to Asia explained why she would uproot her family in obedience to God's call. "While many Americans, even Christians, can't fathom why we would want to take our family overseas, my greatest fear is not having lived the exciting, fulfilling life Christ wants us to live because we weren't willing to give up a few material things along the way. I want to know I have spent my life following His direction, for my sake, for His sake, and for my children's sake. How can I hope my children will follow Him in obedience if I'm not willing to do the same?"

Another spoke to the growing conviction that came with surrender to God's will: "Men of God have challenged me to yield my future, my agenda, and my comfort level to God. As I have done this, my resistance to the urging of God's Spirit regarding international missions diminished, and God has given me peace and a sense of direction and excitement. I believe that God wants me to share His love with people who are as yet unreached with His gospel. I want to obey what He is urging me to do, and I believe He will work out all the details and give more clarity as I follow in faith."

An older missions volunteer found himself on the way to the Middle East after responding to a divine impression: "I was moving up the corporate ladder. We were enjoying life and serving in our local church. My next milestone would be retirement. Following a volunteer mission trip, I was lying in bed thinking about the experience when out of nowhere came a thought, 'We could sell everything, pay off the debt we have and be on the mission field in 30 days if that is what God wanted.' That thought scared me and excited me at the same time. As we prayed about what God would have us to do, our love for missions grew and God confirmed His call."

Another put the relative needs of a church-related ministry in perspective: "I became restless in my church ministry when I realized we were in an extremely church-saturated area. I put out my resume and in interviewing at a rapidly growing church, the pastor mentioned they were located in a high growth area and were competing with many other churches. I became nauseated at the thought of competing with other churches when so many had no opportunity to hear the gospel at all."

A candidate expressed an understanding of why so few hear God's call and are willing to go: "God began to give me an increasing dissatisfaction with the things that this world offers. I began to see how Satan keeps so many Christians inactive and out of his way by just keeping them busy trying to get ahead in this world. Most Christians are not living the abundant life Christ promised because they are unwilling to step out in faith to do what God would have them to do. I decided I wanted to give my life and my family to God to go wherever He chooses to send us."

God especially seems to be stirring this younger generation of students and young people to selflessly and passionately give themselves to something that will make a difference in the world. They want to go to the edge, take a risk, get their hands dirty, and do whatever it takes to introduce a lost world to Jesus. A few years ago we celebrated a record number of collegiate summer missionaries volunteering for overseas assignments. That year 275 were sent to the mission field. Each of the last two years, however, more than 4,000 college students have participated in mission projects through the IMB!

At YouthLink 2000, thousands of high school students were challenged to consider giving their lives to missions in the twenty-first century. Since then, each summer as many as 2,500 young people have had cross-cultural witnessing experiences overseas through M-Fuge, International World Changers, and other volunteer opportunities. It is evident that God is using these experiences to plant a call to missions in their hearts at a formative time when they are making decisions and considering their future vocational choices.

A MISSIONARY-SENDING STRATEGY

This growing interest in missions, and unprecedented doors of opportunity opening all over the world, have combined to expand our vision for mobilizing God's people to impact lostness and reach all peoples for Jesus Christ in this generation. When the active missionary candidate files at the IMB exceeded 3,000, it became apparent that God was moving in the hearts of His people. Southern Baptists had envisioned having 5,000 international missionaries on the field by the end of the year 2000. That goal was not reached until the following year, but once it was, the growth continued to escalate.

More than 1,000 new missionaries were approved and sent to the field each year in 2001 and 2002. Attrition remained static, retirements diminished, and more and more candidates emerged. We had projected that, based on the past 10-year pattern of growth, we would reach 6,000 missionaries in the next seven years. But we were halfway there in only two years when the number of missionaries in active service reached 5,507 in June 2003. If these trends continued, the International Mission Board would have 15,000 missionaries by 2010! Realizing such a growth rate may be unrealistic, various contingencies were taken into consideration. The calculations still projected 8,000 missionaries by the end of the first decade of the twenty-first century if Southern Baptists would provide the support.

In order to fill the strategic personnel needs overseas and accommodate the diversity of those being called to missionary service, alternate categories of service are being provided. Career missionaries have continued to be the primary channel of service with 75 percent of the missionary force appointed for open-ended, long-term assignments. These are people who go to spend their lives on the field. They learn the language, develop an understanding of cultural worldviews, nurture relationships, and engage in long-range strategies for evangelizing the people. Because of the strategic nature of their role in terms of planting and nurturing church growth, discipling and training leaders, and modeling ministries for the indigenous churches of the future,

career missionaries have more stringent educational qualifications and requirements for experience prior to appointment.

It is expected that career missionaries will serve until retirement. However, often there are family and health needs or a sense of God's leadership to a new direction of ministry that may result in missionaries resigning and returning to the United States. The average tenure for those who serve to retirement is 23 years, though many serve 30 to 40 years and longer. Recently two missionary units retired after more than 50 years of active service!

A common misperception is that missionaries who resign are those who have difficulty making adjustments on the mission field. While some do leave the field during their first term, the average tenure of those resigning is more than nine years. This means they are well into their third term of service and have usually been very effective. It is at this point when aging parents at home may need them as caregivers or families are forced to struggle with children going away to boarding school, to college, or other challenges. It was gratifying to see recent research data relative to those resigning in a given year, and 70 percent indicated they would not choose to leave the field but unavoidable needs and circumstances necessitated that decision.

Associate missionaries are those who may not qualify for career appointment due to age or lack of education. But they have extensive professional and church-related ministry experience and are qualified to meet a personnel need that would otherwise go unfilled or divert other missionaries from their primary assignment. Associates are approved for a four-year term, but the assignment can be renewed, and many associate missionaries later fulfill requirements for transferring to career status. Recently the IMB began appointing all long-term missionaries to an initial three-year term as career apprentice missionaries. The apprentice program had previously been designed for those with adequate education and a confirmed calling, but lacking in professional and ministry experience to qualify for appointment. Getting that experience on the mission field under the tutelage of veteran missionaries was felt to be more valuable than work experience in a stateside setting.

The effectiveness of this approach has resulted in all career and associates now being appointed as apprentice missionaries and being mentored and trained on the field. This initial term of service confirms their call to overseas ministry and equips them to assume a significant strategic role following a successful evaluation of their term. Others will sense that their ministry should be based in the States, and they can successfully return to the United States following completion of their three-year commitment without having to resign from missionary service.

In 1965 a two-year opportunity identified as the Journeyman Program was initiated for recent college graduates. This short-term category for single, young adults under 30 years of age has proved to be popular over the years and has continued to grow. God is creating a passion for missions in the hearts of students and as more of them have opportunities to participate in volunteer projects during their college years. Many of them relate to the increasingly youthful global population in countries where young people are interested in meeting Americans and learning English. They are assigned to universities, community ministries, sports evangelism, and many other channels for sharing the gospel with their generation. Others use degrees in teaching or business to assist in teaching missionary kids or helping

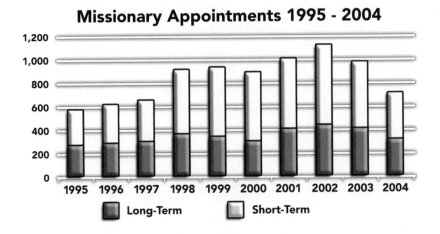

Missionary Appointments 1995 - 2004

Long-Term   Short-Term

on the logistical support teams, while many work alongside other missionaries in evangelism, discipleship, and church planting.

The appeal of the Journeyman Program began to expand as other adults, who were not qualified for career appointment, expressed interest in short-term opportunities. Many felt God was calling them to use their maturity and experience in roles that could benefit the total missions effort and free long-term personnel for more strategic assignments. International Service Corps was designed to provide a channel of service to other qualified, God-called individuals and couples to serve in two- or three-year short-term assignments. Hundreds of Southern Baptists have taken advantage of this opportunity for mission service. Many return for long-term appointment after having fulfilled the qualifications, convicted of God's call to give their lives to reach a lost world. In fact, during the last two years, 43 percent of the career missionaries being appointed had served short-term assignments as journeymen or ISC missionaries.

The interest being expressed by older Southern Baptists to be personally engaged in international missions is a more recent phenomenon. Some express a lifelong call that was never fulfilled, but now in their retirement years they would like to do something related to missions. More and more people are retiring in good health, spiritually mature and desiring to devote their final years to a significant ministry. Others are being led to change careers later in life, and God has laid a call to missions on their hearts.

There is a common theme to their testimonies. As they participated in more and more volunteer trips, the joy and fulfillment of their ministry and witness overseas grew. The appeal of returning home each time to the comforts of home and a routine job continued to diminish. Other mission organizations have seized upon this trend to launch the Finishers' Project, a channel through which retired people could serve and finish life's productive years in missions. As more and more mature Southern Baptists applied to the ISC program, it was decided to create a special category called the Masters Program for those 50 and older to serve for two or three years.

These older, short-term missionaries are bringing a needed maturity and years of professional experience to the field. When linked with the passion, energy, and vision of younger missionary families, they are strengthening our missionary teams and effectiveness. Retirement is not a time for sitting in a rocking chair, playing golf or going fishing when there is a lost world waiting to be won! Gary and Evelyn Harthcock went to Mongolia when they were 71-years-old and continued to renew assignments well into their 80s. Gary said that he did not plan to retire until the devil did, and there was no evidence the devil was planning to retire, so he wasn't either!

In order to train and equip the missionaries who go overseas, the International Mission Board provides four phases of preparation. The first phase is to mentor candidates in the experience and training that will prepare them for missionary service prior to their being approved for appointment. Following appointment, they participate in a seven-week field preparation orientation experience at the Missionary Learning Center near IMB headquarters in Richmond, Virginia. This facility is able to accommodate several hundred missionaries and their families. The learning center is also used for candidate conferences, furlough conferences for veteran stateside missionaries, and other training events. Normally more than 5,000 personnel a year, including children, participate in conferences and events at the center.

4 Phases of Orientation and
7 Dimensions of Field Personnel Competencies

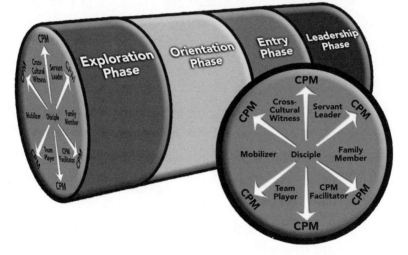

A third on-the-field phase of training and orientation occurs throughout the apprentice term or entire short-term assignment of other personnel when they arrive overseas. The greatest emphasis is placed on language learning and cross-cultural adjustment. The final phase is an ongoing program of life development and continuing education provided by the IMB's International Centre for Excellence in Leadership through self-study courses and modules. Each of the four phases for training missionary personnel is focused on seven dimensions that are the core of missionary competencies. These are (1) discipleship and spiritual growth, (2) servant leadership, (3) cross-cultural witness, (4) family strength and nurture, (5) missions mobilization, (6) facilitator of church-planting movements, and (7) team player.

THE PRIORITY OF AN INCARNATIONAL WITNESS

Why is the basic strategy of the International Mission Board to send and support missionaries when there are so many other things that could be done? Why are we essentially a "missionary-sending agency?" It is because Jesus told us to go. He realized that the personal communication and verbal witness of a Christian living among lost people is the most direct and effective channel of fulfilling our mission. There are many methodologies that can get the gospel to a lost world, and we applaud, support, and engage in many of them. The gospel can be broadcast to millions using media. Bibles and literature can be published and distributed. But Jesus did not tell us to just contribute our monetary support or to find the most cost-efficient way of proclaiming the gospel. He said to go and be His witnesses to the ends of the earth.

When missionaries, or even short-term volunteers, go to plant their lives in a culture and among people who do not know Jesus, the living presence of Jesus Himself goes with them. As they live out their faith through friendships and personal relationships, people can observe the reality of their faith. They gain credibility that allows them to share it verbally. Being there, they can communicate with an understanding of the worldview of the people they live among. They can cultivate a witness, follow up and nurture new fellowships of believers, and walk alongside those God calls out as indigenous local leaders.

We call this an "incarnational witness." It is not only using media tools, humanitarian platforms and occasions for teaching and preaching, but it is allowing nonbelievers to observe in flesh and blood what it means to be a follower of Christ. This is how God revealed Himself to man. Jesus Christ became flesh, enabling the world to behold His glory. We would not presume to approach the uniqueness and significance of Jesus as God incarnate, but the message of Christ is best communicated through the lives of those in whom Christ lives. Many peoples of the world live in places where there are no churches. They do not have access to the Word of God and have never known a

Christian. They are best able to see and understand a Christian witness when one goes and lives in their midst.

What kinds of missionaries are being sent out by the IMB as we envision kingdom growth to the ends of the world? There are some who think that the IMB should appoint anyone in a Southern Baptist church who happens to feel called to missions, without regard to qualifications, and then support them for doing whatever they personally want to do overseas. Relatively few who apply for missionary service are turned down, but we are often criticized for maintaining high standards and criteria in the approval process. Historic phrasing in denominational documents has been retained in guidelines for selective missionary appointment. The IMB is instructed to find, appoint, arrange support for, equip, and send God-called Southern Baptist missionaries who give evidence of piety, zeal for the Master's kingdom, conviction of truth as held by Baptists, and talents for missionary service.[1]

Unlike many mission agencies, we are an entity of our denomination, restricted to sending missionaries from cooperating Southern Baptist churches. Each one approved for appointment must be able to articulate a solid, personal conviction of God's call to overseas service. And with that call is a conviction of gifting for cross-cultural witness and ministry. Those gifts are usually latent, but are stirred by pre-field training, orientation, and equipping, and subsequently by immersion among the peoples to whom one is called.

It would be irresponsible to send into the unsanitary environment and stressful demands of the mission field those who have fragile health, emotional problems, or a record of interpersonal conflict. Character and work references reflect on one's level of maturity and effectiveness and help discern whether a candidate is prepared to move out of the supportive context of a stateside job to a foreign setting. Piety and zeal for the Master's kingdom are indicated by one's growing relationship with Jesus Christ, a sound biblical faith, evidence of disciplined Bible study and prayer, as well as a consistent pattern of witness out of concern for the lost. Candidates must share a common commitment to the global task of the IMB that supersedes the provincialism of their specific assignment.

It has always been expected that missionaries who serve with the IMB have personal convictions of truth that are consistent with those held by Southern Baptists. Some would advocate that missionaries should be supported regardless of what they believe, as if using any doctrinal criteria is an infringement on their freedom and the priesthood of the believer. Individuals can choose to believe what they will, but those representing Southern Baptists and serving with the IMB are accountable to hold and practice doctrinal convictions consistent with the Baptist Faith and Message.

SUPPORTING MISSIONARIES COOPERATIVELY

Sending and supporting missionaries is a ministry assignment given to the International Mission Board by the Southern Baptist Convention on behalf of more than 43,000 churches. In turn, the IMB serves these churches and enables them to impact kingdom growth to the ends of the earth through missionaries who are called out of these local churches. This is done by providing a channel through which they can be equipped, supported, and work together in a structure of mutual accountability.

It is sad that many churches have never had a missionary called to serve overseas from their congregation. For others it has been many years—perhaps even generations—since they have had their own missionary. God's sovereignty is certainly a factor in those who are called. But when the needs of a lost world are so great and it appears so few are hearing that call to go, you have to wonder if the challenge is being presented clearly enough and often enough.

Once a decision to surrender for missions is made, the local church should continue to have a sense of ownership in sending out "their" missionaries. Sending missionaries is a biblical calling of the church, not a denominational agency. When gifts are allocated to the Cooperative Program and given to the Lottie Moon Christmas Offering®, they should be seen as personalized support for the church's missionary as well as for thousands of others. Those churches that do not have missionaries from their congregation are encouraged to adopt missionaries; this helps them to stay informed, be connected, be involved, and have a biblical sense of ownership for sending and supporting missionaries. The IMB exists to assist and serve the churches in this task.

Throughout the history of the Southern Baptist Convention there have been those who have challenged the cooperative principles that enable autonomous churches to work together in missions, evangelism, education, and other ministries. Often the only thing that distinguishes many independent and Bible Baptist churches from the SBC is their unwillingness to work in cooperation with each other. Those outside the SBC often, incorrectly, view the convention with its boards and agencies as a denominational hierarchy that exists to control and manage the work of the churches. In fact, the entities and agencies of the denomination are created and empowered by local churches to serve and facilitate the churches doing more together than they could do separately and individually.

In the nineteenth century T. P. Crawford, a missionary to China, concluded that sending and appointing missionaries through the Foreign Mission Board (as the IMB was known then) was unbiblical. He led most of the North China Mission to secede from the FMB. They eventually returned when the challenge of raising independent support infringed on their missionary work and required a parallel organization in the United States to be set up to raise their support and channel it to the field. There continues to emerge today—even after 160 years of proven effectiveness of cooperative missions—splinter organizations based on the premise that churches should appoint and send their own missionaries instead of working with other churches of like faith and practice to do more than can be done independently. These organizations actually replicate the work of the International Mission Board in providing services such as mobilization and enlistment, orientation and training, coordination of travel and financial services, and directing field strategies.

Many SBC churches support missionaries serving with other organizations. But most provide only a portion of the support for those personnel sent out independently. Many of our largest churches could provide full support for one or more families overseas, but most could not. Most Southern Baptist churches find it difficult to provide support beyond the needs of their own staff and local expenses. However, by churches joining together cooperatively to provide financial support, we are able to send many more missionaries. Missionary families don't have to enlist support directly either. Rather than spending time finding churches to support them—or delaying going to the field until they can find that support—they can trust their needs will be met through the Cooperative Program. Cooperation is biblical, and it empowers kingdom growth!

A church could decide to raise the salary and support of a missionary family and send them out directly. But seldom is adequate orientation and training available in community with others going to the field, such as what missionaries receive at the IMB's Missionary Learning Center. Logistical support is lacking, and churches usually fail to calculate the cost of travel expenses, the shipment of freight, provisions for children's education, medical expenses, insurance to cover major catastrophes and possible medical evacuation if needed, or disability and an adequate pension program. The independent missionary is on his own to obtain a visa or arrange for housing and transportation on the field. Having a global organization such as the IMB to provide these services is a benefit to the churches from which missionaries are called.

Missionaries do not arrive overseas to work isolated and alone. They join a team in a coordinated strategy to impact Unreached People Groups and evangelize their assigned country and population segment. They do not go as "Lone Rangers" to do their thing, oblivious to the calling of colleagues and national partners. They are expected to be accountable to one another and—through the IMB—

to the Southern Baptist churches that send and support them. They are to fulfill their assignment with mutual respect and in cooperation with others as a team that testifies to the common passion for the task. The unity of the Spirit that calls and indwells each one provides a synergy that enables a greater kingdom impact to be made than the sum efforts of many individuals.

Strategic Personnel Deployment

The cooperation, accountability, and mutual respect that is expected of missionaries on the field reflects basic biblical standards for interaction among believers. It is an acknowledgement of the diversity that exists among missionaries and their assignments. Previously Southern Baptist missionaries on the field were a part of large, nationwide organizations that determined the strategies and budgets for everyone working within a specific country. Such structures were bureaucratic and diverted missionary energies to time-consuming administrative tasks and committee responsibilities. These structures usually represented a patronizing, unhealthy parallel with national organizations and created a strain in working relationships with local Baptist partners. In recent years those structures have been dissolved, reducing the amount of missionary manpower that must be given to the mission organization and enabling more personnel to be engaged in the primary task of reaching a lost world.

Missionaries are now organized into local teams focusing on specific people groups, cities, and population segments. There are a small number of logistical support teams to assist in financial services and managing property and travel. Each one is accountable to each other rather than to a hierarchy of administrators. This team structure has decentralized strategic planning to give ownership of strategies to those who actually carry out the work, relate to national partners, and are immersed in the task. Regional leadership teams seek to provide the resources needed and keep the strategy focused on the vision of reaching all peoples through church-planting movements.

Considerable controversy continues to surface as to what a missionary is. Confusion is created as more and more diverse roles emerge. The fact that many cannot be identified as "missionaries" due to serving in restricted countries that prohibit a Christian witness adds to ambiguous perceptions. Some still see missionaries as misfits, out of style and a little out of touch with the real world. Some of them are perceived to have chosen to go overseas because they are not competent for a stateside ministry.

To the contrary, missionaries are attractive, gifted, and engaging individuals, obedient to a God-induced passion for reaching a lost world. They forego most of the amenities and attractions valued by our society. Because our task is unapologetically evangelistic, some perceive missionaries only as preachers who have honed their skills for proclamation and witness in seminary and through years of pastoral experience. While their objective is bringing a lost world to saving faith in Jesus Christ, an in-your-face confrontational witness is seldom effective, and in many parts of the world such public proclamation by foreigners is prohibited. Instead, missionaries live out their witness and find culturally appropriate ways to disseminate the gospel through many diverse assignments and gifts.

Foreign governments often view missionaries as modern colonialists, intent upon destroying cultures and enticing people from their traditional religions, creating conflict in social structures that highly value harmony. Because of that highly inaccurate and outdated perception, many governments forbid missionaries from serving in their countries. At the same time, these nations seek Western aid and request English teachers, health-care specialists, computer programmers, business consultants, and others to accelerate their modernization and development. Missionaries can fill these requests in order to be witnesses in an alien culture, even though they are not identified as missionaries.

Some say that every Christian is to be a missionary where he or she lives. Rather, we are all called to be witnesses and to be obedient to the Great Commission. So, is there a distinction between those who stay at home and those who are led to plant their lives cross-culturally in foreign lands as teachers and doctors, for example? While we all are to be witnesses, missionaries are called to a special role—just as Abraham was called to leave his home and family as an instrument for God that all the nations would be blessed. Paul expressed a special divine calling to take the gospel to the Gentiles and the regions beyond where the gospel was known. But is it imperative that those who respond to such a call be identified as missionaries?

God has never been diverted from His purpose to evangelize a lost world. He has not withdrawn His mandate to disciple the nations. His promise that the gospel eventually will be proclaimed among every nation, people, tribe, and language still holds. Our response in going to the ends of the earth is not qualified by the missionary label, nor are we limited only to places foreign governments welcome traditional missionary personnel. Every church and all of God's people have an obligation to make the gospel known to all peoples by whatever means and channel God provides. The label is not the issue. Being confined to a narrow, traditional concept is not the point. The source of support and the sending agency is irrelevant. A missionary is one who responds to our Lord's mandate to use his gifts, skills, and experience in a cross-cultural setting to share the claims of Christ wherever presence can be legitimately gained, even in a hostile world where missionaries are not welcome.

Where are the missionaries? The International Mission Board does not arbitrarily assign personnel to places and jobs irrespective of their personal sense of call and God's leadership. But missionary candidates are encouraged to consider going to places of high, strategic priority or where the need is most urgent. The lostness and need for Christ is so vast, you could never reach a point of having too many missionaries in any one location. Yet if our task is to reach all peoples, we cannot send all our missionaries to only one part of the world. It is a matter of proportion and priority.

For most of our history Southern Baptists sent missionaries to serve only where missionaries were allowed and welcomed. We became well-acquainted with places such as Spain, Brazil, Nigeria, the Philippines, and more than a hundred countries where our missionaries served openly. But in recent years God has been pushing back the barriers that locked multitudes in spiritual darkness. He is opening innovative channels through which missionaries can gain access to restricted countries and impact Unreached People Groups.

These personnel and their locations usually cannot be identified publicly. It would jeopardize their presence and witness, possibly endanger the safety of their families and expose local believers. They are often identified by an alias, or their initials, and only by the region where they serve. But God knows who and where they are, and they need our prayers. That is why it is more important than ever that churches personalize their involvement by adopting missionaries. They can relate to them through sensitive and secure communication rather than relying on generic information in publications. This might appear to be a bit paranoid, but IMB publications have been found in mosques overseas. Muslim research centers scan the Internet to identify and expose Christian missionaries. Foreign governments hire clipping services to look for any reference to their country and give special attention to church-related publications.

There is a continuing missiological tension between deploying personnel to Unreached People Groups in the Last Frontier and sending missionaries to traditional, historical fields where the harvest is considered to be ripe. By concentrating our resources on the massive unreached populations of China and South Asia—where there are more Unreached People Groups yet to be engaged than in all the rest of the world—are we abandoning responsive fields where the harvest is ripe? Are we wasting personnel and resources in establishing platforms and ministries of sowing in the Muslim world where there is meager response instead of going to open fields where greater evangelistic results can be realized? The answer must be considered from theological, missiological, and practical perspectives.

Theologically, the gospel is the power of God unto salvation. The Spirit of God indwells the message of the gospel to draw all people to Jesus Christ. But response is always dependent on access. As one worker in Northern Africa said, "We have discovered where we sow abundantly, we reap abundantly; where we sow sparingly, we reap sparingly. The only reason we do not have a more abundant harvest in the Muslim world, is that we haven't found a way to sow the gospel more abundantly." Believing God's heart and desire is for all peoples to know and worship Him—and believing in the power of the gospel—we can segment the world into only two parts: current harvest fields and neglected harvest fields.

Missiologically, the task of a missionary is not to always do the job himself. He is to work himself out of a job. We are to proclaim the gospel, win people to Christ, plant churches, train leaders, and move on to the fringes of lostness. There is a principle that characterizes our task—the resources are in the harvest. In other words, winning a lost world is not the exclusive task of Western, cross-cultural missionaries propagating a patronizing dependency on their presence and leadership. The potential for completing the task is represented in the massive numbers of local believers and national churches that join in the task of winning the lost around them and sending out missionaries to neighboring people groups.

In Romans 15:19-21 the apostle Paul said, "from Jerusalem and . . . as far as Illyricum I have fully preached the gospel of Christ. And thus I aspired to preach the gospel, not where Christ was already named . . . but [so] . . . they who have not heard shall understand." He described the missionary task. Not everyone from Jerusalem to Illyricum had been won, discipled, or even heard the gospel. But it had been made accessible to those regions, and churches had been planted to be a nucleus of witness in those locations. Meanwhile Paul went on to regions where people did not yet have access to the gospel.

Missions and evangelism are not synonymous. While evangelism and proclaiming the gospel is the heart and foundation of our missions task, winning as many people to the Lord as possible is not missions. Missions is the task of taking the gospel cross-culturally and geographically beyond where we live to give all peoples the opportunity to hear, understand, and respond in their own cultural context.

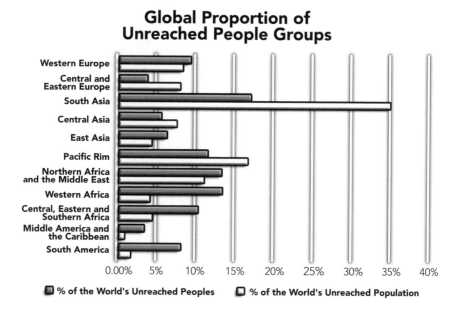

Global Proportion of Unreached People Groups

Categories (top to bottom): Western Europe, Central and Eastern Europe, South Asia, Central Asia, East Asia, Pacific Rim, Northern Africa and the Middle East, Western Africa, Central, Eastern and Southern Africa, Middle America and the Caribbean, South America

Horizontal axis: 0.00%, 5%, 10%, 15%, 20%, 25%, 30%, 35%, 40%

Legend: ◼ % of the World's Unreached Peoples   ◻ % of the World's Unreached Population

Practically, our perception of a harvest field may not be accurate and actually may be distorted by numbers. A large response to the gospel is always contingent upon access and usually upon a long history of witness, plus multiple churches and local believers proclaiming the gospel. Places not considered responsive may be simply places where no one has had an opportunity to hear and understand. As we are told in Romans 10:14, "How then will they call on Him in whom they have not believed? How will they believe in Him whom they have not heard?"

An accurate assessment of harvest and responsiveness is based on how many new believers come to faith in Christ and are baptized relative to the number of believers within a geographic entity or people group. It also takes into account how many new churches are started relative to the number of established churches. A newly reached people group may have only a thousand baptized believers, but in a given period of time may have reached and baptized 10,000 new believers. Another country that has been evangelized and has a million believers may have baptized 20,000 new believers. But the larger number won to Christ is not indicative of a greater responsiveness and harvest.

When we recognize that the resources are in the harvest and that our global missions task is not the unique and exclusive role of our missionaries alone, it is helpful to gain a perspective on where other resources are available in the decision of deploying missionaries and making the gospel accessible to Unreached People Groups. First among these resources are Baptist partners around the world. Where churches have been planted and have grown and matured— and national conventions have been established—they can assume a large part of the responsibility for the task. Our role, in partnership, is to train and encourage them in more of a catalytic role.

Priorities and needs are also affected by the presence of other evangelical believers, churches, and mission agencies. It is foolish to duplicate efforts for building our own kingdom while other parts of the world remain neglected. A third resource is the massive numbers of volunteers being mobilized by our own Southern Baptist churches. Where significant numbers are available, partnering with our missionaries and relating to national churches, methodologies can be developed for evangelism efforts and discipleship training that are no longer dependent upon missionaries. Even people group strategies can be relinquished to stateside church partners and volunteer teams.

One of the factors for determining how personnel should be deployed throughout the world is to identify the unreached and unengaged people groups and where they are located. Priority is given to those with a population greater than 100,000 as well as the unreached and unengaged gateway cities and urban centers, where the greatest concentrations of people live. Another factor is the proportion of lost population relative to Baptist and evangelical resources.

Missionary personnel have a strong sense of call and a passion for their place of service. Why does one go to a place uninvited or live where Christian witness is not welcome? Why does one embrace hardship and danger, subjecting his family to isolation and uncertainty? For the same reason anyone responds to God's call—a passion to reach the lost with the good news of Jesus Christ. Recently the testimony of two missionaries crossed my desk. One is a strategy coordinator focusing on a people group that has never had access to the gospel. The other is a strategy coordinator seeking to reach the lost population segments in a country where missionaries have served for more than 100 years. Both are driven by a passion for people to whom they are called to have an opportunity to know Jesus.

One had gone to the Last Frontier, to a place where evangelism is prohibited, and to people who have been deprived of the gospel. He bemoaned the fact that "many peoples have remained locked in spiritual bondage to their animistic practices for all of history because our traditional approach has been to go only where we were invited." He went on, "The goal of world evangelization is about getting at lostness! It requires more folks who are ready to die . . . in order to go into areas where the gospel hasn't yet penetrated. We must be willing to risk failure, but keep pushing the limits of our ability to go to the edge and mobilize others to do the same. We hear a lot about Muslim extremists, but where are the Christian extremists who have the vision, passion, and drive to go to the hard places?"

The other missionary expressed gratitude for those who had preceded him when the country where he now serves was one of those hard frontier fields. In answer to the question of why God led him to a country where missionaries were welcome and the harvest was plentiful, he said it was because of a "passion and zeal which burns within my breast for the tens of millions who remain unevangelized. Even though I serve on a traditional and open field, few of us live in sheltered environments, protected from harm or persecution. We have gone out with national co-workers to share the gospel and have been threatened, attacked, stoned, and assaulted. I would be willing to lay down my life for the sake of the lost people we are trying to reach. Is the value of a soul in an Unreached People Group any greater than one who has had access to the gospel but has never heard and understood it? The eternity in hell that awaits all without Christ is the same!"

These two missionaries said much more. Their words expressed their vision and their strategy for seeing the Great Commission fulfilled on their field of service. The passion that drives any missionary, whether on a traditional field or the Last Frontier, is the same. It is a passion that flows from the heart of God for a lost and dying world. Those whom God calls are those who are driven to do whatever it takes to see the walls of lostness breached for the sake of the kingdom of God.

These are the ones who say with Isaiah, "Here am I. Send me!" (Isaiah 6:8) in response to the plea of God for someone to go into the darkness. It is not enough to access the lost peoples of the world; we must eradicate the darkness by shining the light of the gospel among all the peoples of the world. There is a pathos in the plea that goes out from missionaries all over the world to mobilize workers, church partners, and intercessors who will share their burden and plead with the Lord of the harvest until the strongholds are destroyed and the kingdom of God has come to the ends of the earth.

[1] Southern Baptist Convention Constitution: Article IX.

CHAPTER SEVEN

JOINING OTHERS IN
KINGDOM PARTNERSHIPS

IMB BASIC ROLE:
To lead and facilitate the international missionary
involvement of Southern Baptists in partnership with overseas Baptists and other Christians who are
fulfilling the Great Commission.

One of my most significant times of encouragement and renewed vision comes in February each year when I have the privilege of joining 20 mission executives in a time of retreat. This group repre-sents the largest evangelical missionary-sending organizations in North America. We often meet at our Missionary Learning Center near Richmond. This annual fellowship always exceeds my own expectations of bonding and mutual support.

Steve Sheldon, the former head of Wycliffe International, and I initiated the retreat during my first year as IMB president. We each had come into our leadership position as a novice administrator about the same time. The IMB was the largest denominational missions agency and Wycliffe the largest para-church agency in the world in terms of sending career missionaries. We felt there was a lot to be gained from a gathering with leaders of other large organizations. There were potentially hundreds of organizations that could have been invited, but in order to facilitate personal interaction and mutual identification, we limited the group to those that were global in their ministry and send and support at least 500 missionary personnel. These were also organizations that were open to cooperation and represented a common kingdom mission of winning a lost world to a saving faith in Jesus Christ.

We come together each year without a predetermined agenda. There is a mutual identification with each other in the unique pressures and challenges each of us faces. In an atmosphere of trust and vulnerability, we have been able to share personally in a way that extends beyond what we can do, even within our own staff. Our vision is enhanced as we discuss strategic issues and pray for each other and for the global challenges we all face. This opportunity for personal, heart-to-heart interaction and communication has resulted in cooperative efforts for impacting Unreached People Groups and accelerating global evangelization without requiring organic unity or infringing on the autonomy of each organization.

One agency allowed us to use their approved, unfilled visa slots in a restricted-access country when we were having difficulty gaining entry. Working together, we have been able to more rapidly expand the translation and use of Campus Crusade's *JESUS* film. We are currently appointing Southern Baptist Bible translators, sent and supported by the IMB but seconded to the Wycliffe organization.

We focus intentionally on the Last Frontier and a mutual commitment to engage all Unreached People Groups. We share data and research, enabling us to avoid duplication and to concentrate our combined efforts more comprehensively. Our strategy coordinators and limited creative access personnel on the field are able to move more rapidly toward the objective of planting Baptist churches when they can call on Pioneers and Operation Mobilization to send in evangelism teams,

Campus Crusade to produce the *JESUS* film, TransWorld Radio and Far Eastern Broadcasting to transmit gospel programs, and Wycliffe to translate and distribute Scripture in the language of the people.

God has raised up within His body many diverse channels for impacting lostness—entities that are committed to the Lordship of Jesus Christ, recognize Jesus as the exclusive and unique Savior of the world, and are committed to discipling the nations and fulfilling the Great Commission. In the same way God gives spiritual gifts to each one in the local church for the completeness of the body, He calls different organizations with unique gifts and ministries to work together in a synergy that will glorify Him and fulfill His mission of evangelizing the whole world. We have seen that the kingdom more rapidly advances when we cease to be concerned about who is in control and who gets credit.

A few years ago a delegation from Wycliffe Bible Translators and the *JESUS* Film Project came to the International Mission Board for several days of consultation. I was asked to drop in and greet these partners with Great Commission organizations. I knew several of the individuals from other meetings and events and cordially welcomed them. I presented my usual update and briefing and wished them a profitable time of interaction. With my closing remark I asked for clarification regarding their meeting. Why were they here?

A spokesman from Wycliffe explained that he and six of his colleagues were with The Seed Company, a new subsidiary of Wycliffe, formed to accelerate the translation of Scripture. I recalled having spoken at the 60th anniversary of the Wycliffe organization a couple of years earlier. As they commemorated 60 years of Bible translation work, they celebrated the fact that the entire Bible had been translated into 394 languages and the New Testament into an additional 903 languages. Then researchers reminded them that there were more than 6,000 languages throughout the world. The impact of that reality cast a pall over the celebratory gathering as they realized it would take another 150 years to get the Bible into the heart language of all the peoples of the world. How many multitudes and generations would die during that time frame without having access to the Word of God?

They realized that they could not continue with business as usual and embraced a vision to have translation projects initiated in every language within the next 25 years. In order to facilitate their contribution to fulfilling the Great Commission and reaching all the peoples of the world as rapidly as possible, they had formed The Seed Company. This was identified as a "renegade" subsidiary that would not be limited to the normal, time-consuming linguistic approach to translation. It would use any means possible to get oral translations of the Gospel of Luke into as many languages as quickly as possible, primarily utilizing native bilingual speakers. This goal was designed to resource the *JESUS* film project, which uses the Gospel of Luke as the text, to accelerate production of this effective evangelistic tool in many more languages.

I was impressed and commended them for their vision and innovative commitment and then asked, "But why are you here this week?" Another of the group explained, "In the early stages of our partnership we realized that unless someone is deliberately engaged in starting churches, the results of our efforts will be rather limited. Having Scripture in their heart language and the *JESUS* film graphically portraying the gospel—especially among oral cultures—is valuable," he continued, "but the lasting benefit will not be significant without follow up being done and local, indigenous churches started." He went on, "And no organization is as focused and effective in church planting as the International Mission Board. Unless you are willing to cooperate in partnership with us, our vision cannot be fulfilled." He added, "Besides, everywhere we get off the plane your people are already there."

It was an emotional moment for me. I was filled with pride that our unique contribution to reaching a lost world was recognized and that our church-planting efforts had a reputation for effectiveness among other evangelical groups. But I was also humbled to realize that God had led us to a strategic focus on church planting and had enabled us to become the largest evangelical missionary-sending organization in the world with personnel extensively deployed around the globe. It wasn't about what we could accomplish for our own credit, but what we could contribute to kingdom growth as a part of a vast array of organizations and agencies God has raised up to reach a lost world.

GREAT COMMISSION PARTNERSHIPS

We had just affiliated with the Evangelical Fellowship of Mission Agencies (EFMA) in 1995 when a Global Consultation on World Evangelization (GCOWE) was held in Seoul, South Korea. The EFMA is a fellowship of about 120 diverse mission agencies. Many are rather small and specialized, but others—both denominational and para-church organizations—are quite large. When the proposal considering membership was presented to our trustees, I asked the EFMA Executive Director, Paul McKaughan, to tell us what would be said about the IMB when we were mentioned in discussions among other mission agencies. He was a bit embarrassed but proceeded to answer my question: "Large, wealthy, independent, exclusive, arrogant. ..." At that point I stopped him and said, "We get the idea!"

A few weeks earlier Avery Willis, Senior Vice President of Overseas Operations for the IMB, made a presentation at the large GCOWE meeting in Korea. He apologized to the more than 4,000 representatives from 186 countries for Southern Baptists' working independently and thinking we could do the job by ourselves because we were so large. He asked forgiveness for our arrogance and acknowledged that if all the peoples of the world are going to hear the gospel, we are going to have to work together. He went on to pledge our cooperation in the effort to complete the Great Commission and distributed our people group research database that had previously been used exclusively by the IMB. It totally revolutionized attitudes and relationships among Baptist partners and groups all over the world who had seen us as aloof and self-sufficient.

Years ago an effective witnessing tool called chronological Bible storying gained widespread popularity, especially among nonliterate tribal groups. Although several organizations had begun using this approach, New Tribes Mission, which worked with many isolated, nonliterate tribes, was most prominent. They developed a systematic approach to present the Bible in the narrative pattern of oral cultures. They readily shared their system with other organizations that translated the material and adapted it to other oral cultures. Not only did the storying approach give people a thorough understanding of God, man's sin, and the need of a Redeemer through the stories of the Old Testament, they were a form of communication that could be readily shared among the people themselves.

As evangelical organizations began to focus on the Last Frontier people groups who had yet to hear and respond to the gospel, an amazing reality surfaced. Most of them were oral cultures, people who could not read or understand the Bible and evangelistic literature, even if it had been available in their own language. It was the reason many of them remained unreached. Since most of our mission strategies are geared to the Bible and to using the written word for discipleship, leadership training, and church planting, we found that we were ill-equipped for reaching these nonliterate people groups.

Chronological Bible storying could be used to share the gospel, but how could discipleship and the training that is needed for church-planting movements take place? The challenge was bigger than any one organization, but four of the largest mission agencies found themselves at the forefront of meeting this need. The International Mission Board, Campus Crusade for Christ, Wycliffe Bible Translators and Youth With a Mission were all significantly engaging oral cultures and people groups. Working together in what has come to be called OneStory (formerly known as the Epic Partnership), oral materials are being developed and shared for discipleship and leadership training based on the narrative approach of chronological Bible storying.

Duplication is avoided, the provision of materials for people groups all over the world is being accelerated, and other mission agencies are being served by these cooperative efforts.

Cooperation neither requires one to compromise doctrinal positions nor to sacrifice convictions concerning methodology, because cooperation and unity is not an end in itself. Cooperating with others is a utilitarian approach to accomplish a mutual objective. But there must be parameters to any partnership. When various organizations come together, seeking to impact the lostness of Unreached People Groups, a synergy can result that makes the gospel known on a broader scale than if one were trying to do it alone.

Ecumenism implies an organic unity in which each participating entity gives up something for the sake of unity. Southern Baptists would never select unity over doctrinal convictions based on the inerrant Word of God. We would never compromise essential matters of faith for a utilitarian objective. But we have seen that cooperation with others can provide an opportunity for doctrinal influence and leadership. Even Baptists have a broad diversity of beliefs and practices; it takes more than a common name to reflect doctrinal conformity and spiritual convictions that are true to the Word of God.

Years ago when I was coordinating our work in India, our personnel were quite limited. We sought opportunities for volunteers and itinerant missionaries to come to India for only a limited time to partner with local Baptists in evangelism and leadership training. Our travel and research had discovered 28 distinct Baptist unions and associations in the country. Many of them were localized in certain geographic areas, but others were quite extensive. Some had come into existence through the work of British or American Baptists and even dated back to the time of missionary William Carey, who went to India in 1793. Others were started by independent evangelists or Indian believers who traveled abroad and were introduced to the Baptist faith.

It was disconcerting to find that many had succumbed to liberal influences through the generations and, though they called themselves

Baptists, their faith and practices represented no similarity to the biblical faith we embraced as Southern Baptists. I found other groups of churches and associations that had neither heard the name Baptist nor had any historical connection with Baptists. Yet their beliefs were based on the New Testament, and they were identical to us in faith and practice. I sought the advice of the overseas leadership at the International Mission Board at the time and asked, "Should we partner with groups who call themselves 'Baptist' but are not, or should we work with those who are identical to Baptists in what they believe but are not identified as Baptist?" The ambiguous reply was that such discernment and decisions would have to be made on the field.

We have continued to partner in close working relationships with evangelicals of like faith and practice, even as we continue to work primarily with other Baptists. Our influence toward sound doctrine has been significant. However, the primary focus of our mission task is not other Christian groups. It is relating to a lost world and to those who do not know Christ.

We are often asked why we cooperate with some groups and not with others. The Chinese have an expression: "You cannot clap with one hand." Just as it takes two hands to applaud, it takes two parties committed to cooperation for cooperation to occur. If one seeks to undercut the support and credibility of the other, it inhibits the ability to work together for a common objective. We can affiliate with other organizations and fellowships globally and locally, but there have to be parameters.

We cannot allow our cooperation in common mission efforts to imply an endorsement of others and what they believe if those beliefs go beyond that with which we can be identified. "Unity in diversity" appears to be a noble slogan, but one cannot compromise important scriptural teachings for the sake of unity. For example, Southern Baptists do not choose to be a part of the World Council of Churches. The diversity of doctrine, programs, and policies is too great and beyond that with which we can identify. In order to establish guidelines for cooperation, the International Mission Board has identified five levels of partnership. Some partnerships are temporary, while others are ongoing relationships. Many barely represent a relationship at all, but are two groups with a common objective who happen to be aware of each other and have some degree of communication and fellowship in a common arena of work.

Five Levels of Partnership

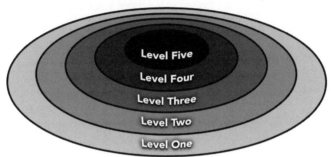

LEVEL ONE is the most superficial level of partnering and is very broad. Its aim is to gain initial access to a people group or population segment. The primary principle is acceptability of the people to be reached. Creativity and flexibility are essential as a missionary tries to make inroads into what may be a hostile situation. Cooperation may be with a local university or medical facility that has no Christian or religious identification whatsoever. Government officials have enabled educational programs and social ministries to provide access to a previously closed country. These partnerships are with gatekeepers and those who have influence in society. IMB personnel have utilized a link with secular, humanitarian organizations and multinational corporations to gain access. Once local relationships and legal presence are established, we move beyond the partnership to fulfill our own agenda.

LEVEL TWO takes one's ministry to the next strategic step. The purpose of cooperation at this level is to open the door to the gospel and make an impact on society. It requires many partners and organizations, each doing their own thing—not necessarily as a part of a unified organization. In many parts of the world strategic alliances have been formed to coordinate the work of multiple agencies and organizations. In enlisting prayer for a people group or city, one would not limit prayer to our own churches or denomination. A partnership may generate an advocacy network far beyond our own realm of contacts.

Responding to a natural disaster, addressing chronic famine, or providing pure drinking water can make an impact. The partnership may include anyone who wishes to address these needs and is equipped to contribute to them. We have had a considerable role in relief efforts in the United States and overseas by partnering on occasion with the International Red Cross or the United Nations High Commission for Refugees. Due to the credibility of these relationships, our access and impact has extended far beyond the immediate needs met by these cooperative projects. If the IMB had not been a part of a larger cooperative effort, we may have missed the opportunity to have been involved in helping meet common goals.

LEVEL THREE takes the partnership beyond prayer advocacy, humanitarian projects, or involvement with government and secular institutions to a point of gospel presentation. Therefore, partners at this level must be defined by those committed to New Testament evangelism. The number of potential partner organizations is greatly reduced to those that are devoted to presenting Jesus Christ as the exclusive way of salvation and that believe the only hope for eternal life is coming to Him in repentance and faith as Savior and Lord. Baptists are not the only ones who believe this and are seeking to communicate this good news to a lost world. God has called out many evangelicals who are devoted to the primary purpose of proclaiming the gospel. We are not in competition with anyone else seeking to win a lost world to Jesus Christ. We may not agree with their methodology and cannot endorse other things for which their organizations stand. We are not likely to subsume our organizational accountability and effectiveness to a unified effort. But at this level of partnership we may encourage and facilitate others working alongside us to make a greater impact on lostness beyond what our limited number of personnel can do.

Many organizations are devoted to the production of specialized tools and resources that can be used by others, such as those who produce and broadcast radio programs, publish gospel literature, develop films and other media tools. There are agencies that mobilize vast numbers of short- and long-term personnel for the sake of saturation gospel impact such as Operation Mobilization, Youth With a Mission, Campus Crusade for Christ and others. Frontiers and Arab World Ministries focus on reaching the Muslim world. Sudan Interior Mission and African Inland Mission concentrate on penetrating Africa, while the Latin America Mission, Greater Europe Mission, and Overseas Missionary Fellowship target specific areas to which they have been called. Working separately or together, the gospel is being made known, the seeds are being planted, and hearts are prepared for the harvest.

LEVEL FOUR of partnerships moves beyond evangelism and proclamation. Having made the gospel accessible to lost population groups, they move to the stage of church planting. Obviously at this level the scope of potential partners is greatly reduced and limited to those that are compatible with Baptist doctrine. The many Christian agencies, churches, and individuals that support evangelism or engage in humanitarian work without regard for starting churches are less helpful at this level. Likewise, many Protestant denominations or nondenominational agencies that enlist personnel from many various streams of church backgrounds would be unacceptable partners. Some come from traditions that do not represent a New Testament church model, do not advocate believers' baptism, or give undue emphasis to specific spiritual gifts. While there are many independent groups and evangelical organizations that are doctrinally sound and compatible with what we believe as Baptists, our partnership in church planting gravitates toward national Baptist partners. This level may also include international agencies that have specialized roles in providing resources and opening doors of opportunity so that we can follow up their efforts with a focus on planting churches that are Baptist.

Earlier we discussed the phenomenal growth in India that had occurred as a result of medical and agricultural ministries. Other organizations played a significant role in the church planting that Baptist missionaries and evangelists were able to do. An organization called Gospel Recordings produced a simple tape player and evangelistic tapes in local languages that were used extensively in the villages. Campus Crusade teams saturated the area with showings of the *JESUS* film. As the team would move on to a subsequent location, our Baptist evangelists, with the help of Campus Crusade, would follow up with those who indicated an interest in the gospel, begin Bible study groups, and start Baptist churches. TransWorld Radio was a strategic partner in broadcasting the gospel in the tribal languages of Orissa that resulted in a church-planting movement emerging among the Kui people there.

LEVEL FIVE is the point at which the missionary's aim is to create ongoing structures and institutions that will shape the future of Christianity among a people and assure its continuing extension to the fringes of lostness. These structures would include leadership training, discipleship programs, and missionary-sending structures that should not be dependent on an outside missions agency. Because these programs have implications beyond the involvement of the IMB and our missionary personnel, the governing principle of partnership must be narrowly focused. Nothing less than uncompromising commitment to doctrinal orthodoxy is acceptable.

Among the most valuable partners at this level are Southern Baptist seminaries. Most of them have established partnerships with overseas seminaries and are able to contribute to quality academic programs beyond what the IMB is equipped to do. A few years ago we sought to enhance this partnership by initiating "Seminary Professors Abroad." The IMB covered the cost of teachers from SBC seminaries traveling overseas to teach in seminaries. Scholarships to international students have equipped national leaders and assured the quality of indigenous institutions. National conventions have looked to personnel and resources from other Baptist bodies to expand and supplement what Southern Baptists are able to do. For example, missionaries from Korea are training pastors in Central Asia, and missionaries from Brazil are working in Angola, Mozambique, Morocco, and other fields around the world.

These five levels of relationships are not always explicit and are not intended to be exhaustive. But they illustrate the partnerships with which we are engaged to fulfill the Great Commission. The task of discipling the nations and peoples of the world is not ours alone. It must be carried out in harmony with other evangelical believers rather than in isolation. To work independently in exclusion of others would not mean greater effectiveness. It would marginalize Southern Baptists from being aligned with much of what God is doing in the world.

God's kingdom is bigger than Southern Baptists, and while we hold firmly and without compromise to the Baptist Faith and Message, cooperation with the efforts of others is accelerating kingdom growth, especially in places that have previously not had access to the gospel. Such cooperation must not infringe on the autonomy of mission partners in following God's leadership and our accountability to Southern Baptists. It must be based on a mutual trust and commitment to a common objective.

PARTNERSHIP WITH OVERSEAS BAPTISTS

One of the most gratifying aspects of partnership in international missions is the joy of relating to more than 150 overseas Baptist conventions, unions, and associations around the world. While more and more IMB personnel are being assigned to the last frontiers of lostness where there are no Baptist churches and Christian believers, historically most have worked in partnership with local churches in countries where believers have been organized into cooperative fellowships of conventions and unions of their own. Many Southern Baptists perceive our evangelism and church planting overseas to be an extension of the Southern Baptist Convention. In fact, I am often asked, "How many Southern Baptist churches do we have in Brazil (or some other country)?" The answer is none! Southern Baptist churches are limited to those within the United States who choose to affiliate with the SBC.

Baptist churches around the world relate to their own local conventions and national entities—such as the Argentina Baptist Convention, Nigeria Baptist Convention, or German Baptist Union—with full autonomy and responsibility for their cooperative ministries. Some, such as in Canada and the Philippines, have chosen to call their conventions Southern Baptist. This is not because of any formal relationship with the SBC, but due to historic ties or in order to identify with the doctrinal and evangelistic principles that characterize this identity.

Formation of national conventions overseas is an appropriate outgrowth of effective mission work. As churches increase in number, it is normal for them to work together and take responsibility to support various institutions and ministries. They recognize they can do together what individual churches cannot do alone. The formation of local associations—and subsequently nationwide conventions—has been an objective of church-planting efforts, but the IMB does not represent any authority over these entities.

In recent years we participated in celebrating the 50th anniversary of many Baptist conventions that resulted from the post-World War II expansion of missionary efforts. But there are many conventions that have been in existence much longer. In 1999 I had the privilege of attending the 150th anniversary of Baptist work in Nigeria where there are now more than a million members in more than 7,000 churches. Not all the conventions and unions with which we partner overseas were started by Southern Baptists. The Baptist Union of Sri Lanka recently commemorated its 190th anniversary, as it was begun by British Baptists long before the Southern Baptist Convention came into existence.

Missionaries do not have a patronizing leadership role among Baptist partners that are now assuming responsibility for their own programs and strategies, even in places where missionaries may have begun the work. Some missionary personnel serve in countries where they were invited to join in the work and assist existing Baptist conventions or associations. Some have specialized assignments, but usually the partnership exists to assist the churches in evangelistic outreach and enhance church planting in new areas. Annual statistics reported by the IMB do not represent the exclusive work of American missionaries, but are reflective of our partnership with affiliated Baptist entities overseas. Reports include only those entities where IMB personnel are currently involved.

We have rejoiced to see national leadership trained and assuming positions of leadership responsibility, allowing missionaries to be redeployed to the cutting edge of lostness. Missionary personnel continue to be assigned to hospitals, seminaries, and publication ministries, not because of dependency on them, but as an asset and affirmation of our partnership in the total work of the local churches. Leadership training beyond residential seminaries and Bible schools, discipleship programs and the training of indigenous missionaries for cross-cultural ministry have continued to be among the primary partnership roles of IMB personnel in working with overseas Baptist partners. In recent years the IMB has been able to move beyond working with established churches and give greater priority to spreading the gospel where there are no churches.

A greater emphasis is being placed on mobilizing the 98,561 Baptist churches with which we are affiliated to send and support their own missionaries. In 2003, Baptist conventions and unions where Southern Baptists have missionaries sent and supported 1,901 international missionaries. An additional 3,920 cross-cultural home missionaries were supported by these conventions to target unreached and under-evangelized people groups within their own countries.

We are often asked why the International Mission Board doesn't support these missionaries. We are one of the few mission agencies in North America that sends and supports only American missionaries. As an agency of the SBC our responsibility and ministry assignment is to send and support missionaries called out of our churches. Since churches overseas are not a part of the SBC, we are not authorized to support those of other nationalities, nor have Southern Baptist churches provided the financial resources to do more than support our own personnel.

But the primary reason is that we should not deprive Korean Baptists, Filipino Baptists, and others from being obedient to the Great Commission and having the joy of calling out and sending their own missionaries. Their churches are strengthened by sharing that responsibility and gaining a sense of ownership of their own mission programs and involvement. They would not fully mature as New Testament churches were someone else to underwrite the support of their missionaries.

One of the most prominent areas of partnership emerging with overseas Baptists is our participation in training and orienting national missionaries. We also assist with platforms and logistical arrangements on the fields where they serve. It is not unusual to find a Brazilian missionary on the team with IMB personnel in Northern Africa or Korean and Filipino missionaries serving with Southern Baptists on a team in East Asia. In fact, missionaries from other countries have many advantages compared to Americans: they do not have the same high profile and are able to blend in more inconspicuously with the people. In 1999 the IMB sponsored a series of consultations with Baptist leaders and representatives from national conventions and unions in various areas of the world. Designated as AWE conferences—Advancing World Evangelization—these consultations were successful in strengthening communication and relationships, sharing our vision for bringing all the peoples of the world to saving faith in Jesus Christ, renewing our commitment to partnership, and challenging these Baptist partners to join us in the mission task.

Lest anyone have the impression that the International Mission Board has a unique relationship—or even some degree of authority over Baptist churches overseas—it should be clarified that local churches and conventions, consistent with our Baptist polity and doctrine, are completely autonomous. As such, they have the freedom to relate to other organizations and other Baptist mission groups. Their bilateral relationship with the International Mission Board is not an exclusive one. Many Southern Baptists have been to Kenya on volunteer mission trips and have been assisted by Southern Baptist missionaries while relating to churches and national pastors. But they may not be aware that the Kenyan Baptist Convention has relationships with more than 30 distinct Baptist missions agencies other than the IMB.

We have been thrilled with the opportunity that has opened in the former Soviet Union during the last 15 years. But we are not the only ones working with the Russian Baptist Union. Multiple partners including the European Baptist Federation, Slavic Gospel Union, and others are starting churches, training pastors, and assisting the Baptist Union throughout the country and in other republics. As many as 12 different missions agencies are working with the same Baptist convention we relate to in Japan, and this is true in other countries as well.

STATESIDE KINGDOM PARTNERS

Empowering kingdom growth means serving other organizations and entities and facilitating their involvement in reaching a lost world. It has already been noted that missionaries with the International Mission Board are spread pretty thin. But the potential for extending the kingdom of God to the ends of the earth is enhanced through mobilizing churches, denominational entities, and independent Southern Baptist organizations. In addition to the many evangelical denominations and para-church missions agencies seeking to take the gospel to the nations, there are many independent groups that have been organized by individuals with a heart for missions to promote specific strategies or partnership missions in certain areas of the world. Full-time evangelists are spending more time than ever before in campaigns overseas. They enlist volunteer teams and report a significant harvest on responsive fields where the gospel can be shared openly.

We have identified 53 such organizations among Southern Baptists alone. Although they are not affiliated with the Southern Baptist Convention, they wave their banner of Southern Baptist identity with pride. Each has been called and organized for a unique strategy. Many have a limited role in a few specific countries, while others have more widespread engagement. Because the International Mission Board has the assigned responsibility for work of the SBC overseas, an attitude sometimes emerged in the past that no one should be involved overseas unless it was under the auspices of the IMB. Meanwhile, more and more Americans traveled abroad. As internationalization of commerce expanded exposure to our world, God moved in the hearts of many individuals to respond to opportunities for ministry and evangelistic witness overseas.

With an interest in finding out what other Southern Baptists were doing, we convened a gathering of evangelists and various organizations to establish communication and understanding. It was impressive as they shared the compelling burden God had laid on their hearts and how He had opened doors of opportunities to which they had responded. After a couple of days of sharing, we asked what the IMB could do to facilitate and assist in what God was leading them to do. There was a moment of disbelief as they processed the fact they were not being criticized for working independently. Then they responded. Without exception, the representative of every group said, "We want you to help us so that what God has led us to do can be an asset to your missionaries and can fit with the strategies of the IMB." These groups had organized into a "Fellowship of Baptist World Ministries" and continue to be valuable partners in mobilizing volunteers and implementing overseas projects that are making an impact on lostness far beyond what our missionaries can do.

One of our most valuable partnerships has been with state conventions and local associations as their roles in missions have grown. Rather than relegating reaching the ends of the earth to a denominational missions agency, these entities are able to mobilize churches, promote missions support, and facilitate overseas involvement in a synergy of cooperation. Associations are focused on local needs and mission opportunities, and state conventions are concerned about nurturing and equipping their churches to reach the people and communities within their state. However, both recognize the importance of giving their churches a vision for the whole world and being a channel to facilitate global involvement. Missions is reaching beyond where one lives geographically and culturally. Just as churches lose their vitality when they become self-centered and inwardly focused, so do other entities when they neglect the larger mission task of mobilizing the people of God to reach a lost world.

For years, established state conventions have been linking with new-work states to accelerate and strengthen our Baptist witness and growth in pioneer areas of the United States and Canada. It has been gratifying to see how state conventions have also worked with the International Mission Board to form overseas partnerships with countries, national conventions, and people groups. These partnerships are usually for three years, but it is hard to bring them to closure once relationships are established and the needs of the overseas churches are deeply implanted in the hearts of the stateside partner. State Baptist papers keep missions before their readers as they profile volunteer teams and projects and, in so doing, promote the Great Commission and the work of our missionaries.

Without the aid of state conventions, it would be impossible for the IMB to enlist the thousands of volunteers who are participating in evangelism crusades, disaster relief, ministry projects, sports outreach, construction, medical work, and a multitude of other areas of witness around the world. They have set up mission partnership offices and staffed them to assist in this task. They mobilize the volunteers, provide orientation and training, and vastly increase the potential of Southern Baptists being on mission with God.

It is sometimes disconcerting when these partnerships become independent and move away from sound mission strategies, but the good that is done surpasses the few detrimental projects and the occasional dependency that is created. The work of the International Mission Board is more effective, the global harvest is accelerated, a lost world is hearing the gospel, and the kingdom of God is being advanced because state conventions, associations, and other stateside partners are working together cooperatively.

We have discovered that when we cease to be concerned about who gets credit and who is in control, we are amazed at what God does among us. He will not share His glory. Those who work for recognition of their own efforts, seek to claim credit for what they have done, or work for the acclaim of their own success, will not receive the anointing of God's power. The amazing statistical growth we have been able to report in recent years cannot be credited to the work and strategies of the IMB, but only to a movement of God who desires to be exalted among all peoples.

We can report evangelistic harvest and church growth overseas related to our own work because of effective partnerships with national conventions and churches with which we are affiliated. Spiritual breakthroughs are occurring on previously restricted fields because of a network of Great Commission agencies that are working together to impact the lostness of our world. In fact, the greatest threat to our effectiveness is the tendency to take pride in what we have done rather than being humbled and recognizing that whatever we are able to do is due to God's grace and blessing.

Isaiah reminds us that God will not give His glory to another (Isaiah 42:8). And Proverbs 16:18 tells us, "Pride goes before destruction, and a haughty spirit before stumbling." I must confess that I am not guiltless in this regard. In fact, I am probably most vulnerable as I seek to share with Southern Baptists what the IMB is doing. Record numbers are not the point. Statistical growth is not the objective. Being a large denomination and missions agency and annually comparing ourselves to what we did last year, or during the past 10 years, only encourages us to commend ourselves by ourselves (2 Corinthians 10:12), rather than simply being faithful in all that God wants to do through us and giving Him the glory!

Perhaps we have not moved more consistently toward our visionary goals of reaching all peoples because God knows our tendency to take pride in what we have done. Our greatest danger of forfeiting what God would choose to do through us may be our sinful tendency of self-glory in taking credit for what God has done. God alone is worthy of all honor and praise and will not share His glory. He has blessed Southern Baptists in numbers and resources, not so that we can be a great denomination, but in order to have a significant role in His plan and purpose to reach the nations. It is not an exclusive role that belongs only to us, but it appears that He has ordained us to have a significant piece of the action. May we be found faithful in serving His kingdom in a humble servant role that we might proclaim with others, "To God be the glory, great things He has done!"

CHAPTER EIGHT

THE CHALLENGE OF COMMITMENT
TO KINGDOM GROWTH

SBC MINISTRY ASSIGNMENTS TO THE IMB

- **Assist churches** by evangelizing persons, planting Baptist churches, and nurturing church-planting movements among all people groups outside the United States and Canada.

- **Assist churches** in sending and supporting Southern Baptist missionaries and volunteers by enlisting, equipping, and enabling them to fulfill their calling.

- **Assist churches** and partners to mobilize Southern Baptists to be involved in international missions through praying, giving, and going.

- **Assist churches** in fulfilling their international missions task by developing global strategies, including human need-based ministries, and providing leadership, administrative support, and financial accountability.

Pastor Bob had been at Calvary Baptist Church for almost 10 years. He had pastored three other churches following graduation from seminary before coming to Calvary. The first was a small rural church that had little potential for growth but had provided valuable experience in learning to relate to people with sensitivity and in sharpening his pastoral and preaching skills. He had a good tenure and effective ministry in his next two churches. The first was a small congregation in a large town with several other Southern Baptist churches. The second was a newer church in the suburbs of a large city that experienced significant growth under his leadership.

In both of these situations the fellowship was good, his family was loved and well-cared for, and the congregations were open to innovative programs and leadership. Bob was able to train and motivate the people for evangelistic outreach, and both churches grew under his strong, Bible-based preaching. Especially in the more recent suburban pastorate, Bob's reputation spread as membership increased and new building programs were initiated. Opportunities to serve on denominational committees and boards broadened his experience and notoriety.

The call to Calvary was not a surprise. A number of pastor-search committees had been in contact with Bob, though he had struggled to determine whether or not it was God's will to respond and make the move. There was a desire to stay where he was as he could envision continuing growth and a very satisfying ministry. His family had settled in and felt comfortable in the community. But there was something that went back to the heart of Bob's call to the ministry that could be interpreted only as a passion to make the greatest impact possible for the sake of God's kingdom. He realized Calvary would provide that opportunity.

The membership and potential resources were much larger, but he would be making a long-term commitment. So the decision had better be right. He was plagued by questions about whether or not his leadership style was a fit and would be accepted. He also entertained anxious thoughts about whether he would soon be overwhelmed by the demands of a larger church and find himself longing to return to the secure and comfortable environment of his present pastorate. Several circumstances and issues converged, including advice from close friends and colleagues, which finally convinced Bob and his wife, beyond all doubt, that God was calling them to Calvary.

The first few years were challenging and, at the same time, exhilarating. He arrived on the crest of a wave of growth. They were located on the fringe of massive new housing developments, and young families were joining the church regularly. God blessed in adding new staff who were filled with fresh, visionary ideas yet blended well with older, tenured associates. Bob was especially pleased to find that he could pour more of himself into preaching and relinquish time-consuming administrative responsibilities and pastoral roles. He enjoyed coordinating the various programs and ministries and keeping the vision of the church focused. This was especially significant since they had begun to televise their services on the local cable network and expand the witness and impact of the church.

Things went well for several years, but then Bob began to sense the vibrancy and excitement beginning to diminish. It was barely noticeable at first. Attendance was strong, and baptisms and other additions continued at impressive levels. All the programs were clicking along successfully, but something seemed to be lacking. It became evident when, for the first time in Bob's tenure, budget problems developed. An ambitious building program had over-extended the church's resources. A number of older families who disagreed with the new facilities and indebtedness left the church. In the past little had to be said about church programs and activities, as they seemed to generate interest and involvement in themselves. But now more and more promotion was needed just to sustain attendance and commitment.

Bob had always been conscientious about the larger mission task of the church. In all the churches he pastored, he had encouraged strong support for mission offerings, insisting the church maintain a tithe of undesignated receipts, or 10 percent, to the Cooperative Program. However, that had been cut to 5 percent for the last two years because of the financial squeeze, but with the assurance that the cutback was only temporary.

Because of the demands on him as the pastor of a growing church, Bob had never been personally involved in significant mission experiences away from home. He was very active in the local association and had led Calvary to assume the primary role in starting a new church a few years earlier. He had been on a preaching crusade to Brazil during his previous pastorate and accompanied a team from his church on a mission trip to Mexico a couple of years ago. But apart from participating in a disaster relief project following a hurricane in a neighboring state, he had not had time for other mission trips. Conferences, denominational responsibilities and needed vacations—often used for developing preaching plans—took him out of the pulpit as much as he felt he could afford. However, he did encourage other staff to organize and mobilize members for mission projects, primarily as a part of his state convention's partnership with a pioneer state in the Midwest and an occasional overseas trip. He always gave personal attention and endorsement to the projects.

Bob's perspective and attitude toward missions began to change when a close friend and neighboring pastor came back from a vision trip to China. He shared enthusiastically how it had impacted his life and literally revolutionized the vitality of his church. Always one on the lookout for something that worked—and willing to learn from the example of others—Bob was intrigued and responded to the encouragement of his friend to go on an overseas vision trip.

As the time approached, the information he received made it apparent that he would be traveling into an area where missionaries had never been allowed and foreigners were viewed with suspicion. Bob began to wonder what he had gotten into and contemplated how he might get out of his commitment. But in the end he went. In spite of the long travel and jet lag, Bob enjoyed the fellowship with other pastors. He knew several casually and found a real camaraderie as they shared the similar experiences and challenges of their churches and talked about current denominational issues.

Bob would never have identified himself as provincial. Though he had not traveled extensively, there were vacations to Hawaii and

Europe, the one-time mission trips to Brazil and Mexico and a tour to Israel. He considered himself knowledgeable and somewhat cosmopolitan, but admittedly had not paid much attention to what was going on in missions around the world. He was aware of getting material from the International Mission Board and always intended to read it, but it usually got lost in the volume of accumulated mail that was eventually discarded.

Each time he would pause and look at the cover of *The Commission* magazine, or see a press release about the report of a missionary somewhere in the world, there was something that would attract his attention and interest. But there was also a subtle conviction that if he took time to read it, he would come away with a sense of responsibility he wasn't ready to face. After all, he had enough to do in leading a growing church, impacting a large city, and feeding his people spiritually. He just didn't have the margin for assimilating anything else, especially something on the other side of the world.

However, something changed dramatically as he participated in a trip to what the IMB called the Last Frontier of the Great Commission. Bob was assigned with another pastor to a strategy coordinator for a people group that had never heard the gospel. At first, Bob was incredulous that there could be anyone anywhere in this age of modern communication and technology who had never heard of Jesus. But he found himself in a large city where there were no churches and in a country that had prohibited any missionary presence. As they encountered people on the streets and in public places, he at least wanted to give them a Bible or gospel tract and was startled to find the Bible had never been translated into the language of the people. No one had bothered to publish tracts or evangelistic material for these people. As he observed animistic rituals and superstitions that seemed to hold the people in bondage, the initial curiosity and culture shock he had felt began to turn into grief and compassion.

Hope emerged as he had the opportunity to meet with some secret believers and hear their testimonies of faith. There was a thrilling leap in Bob's spirit as they expressed such confidence in God and boldness in their witness, in spite of harassment and persecution. He felt a compulsion to come alongside them and encourage them. Bob thought of the resources that his church represented and, for the first time, he realized that most of them had been focused on the self-interest of local programs and facilities, while places like this continued to be neglected. Not waiting to return home and confer with his staff, Bob assured the strategy coordinator of his commitment to partner with him to do whatever his church could to evangelize this people group.

Neither Bob's church, nor Bob himself, was prepared for the emotion that would characterize the report of his trip. Tears flowed freely as he tried to portray in words the lostness of the people he had visited. They readily accepted his recommendation to adopt this people group and partner with the IMB and missionaries assigned to reach them with the gospel. A prayer team was organized to enlist and encourage prayer and to keep information about the people flowing to the congregation. Within a few months a strategy team was organized to be a point of contact with the missionary partners and establish contact with other mission agencies that were engaging this people group. A survey team from the church made a trip to the region and did extensive research regarding the people, the demographics, the political situation, social characteristics, and specific needs through which a door of ministry might be opened.

Within the following year, three different teams had made trips to prayerwalk among the cities and towns, praying for the government leaders and interceding for the people, as well as seeking God's leadership for what the church could do. The strategy coordinator discovered the local universities would like Americans to come and teach English. Calvary Baptist Church was able to enlist several teachers and educators to spend a month during the next summer on-site in these projects. As they bonded with the students and professors, they saw several pray to receive Christ as Savior. Testifying of these breakthroughs encouraged the church back home, and more and more members of the congregation became conscientious about praying for "their people."

A businessman with a multinational corporation found that his company was opening a branch in the city where this people group was located, and there was a possibility of his being assigned there. Meanwhile, the local missionary team had been able to begin radio broadcasts in the language of the people with the help of the church. One of the biggest challenges Calvary faced was raising 25,000 dollars to underwrite the translation and production of the *JESUS* film in the language of their people. There was only a slight hesitation because budget receipts were still running behind and the building indebtedness continued to loom. But when the amount was exceeded in one special offering, Pastor Bob and the congregation began to realize that God was moving in a special way. The most exciting day anyone can remember at Calvary—among the constant flow of special events and programs—was when it was announced that the first church had been started among their people group.

For the first time in Bob's pastoral ministry, young people and even some adults began to commit to missionary service. Volunteer teams returned from projects overseas realizing they ought to be doing at home what they went overseas to do. People filled leadership needs in the church that had gone vacant for extended periods of time. The numbers participating in visitation began to grow. A marked increase in professions of faith and baptisms occurred as more members became conscientious about witnessing to lost neighbors and co-workers.

Calvary had always had an effective youth ministry, but there was frustration that once their young people went off to college and left the supportive environment of their youth group, many dropped out of church. Now they discovered a new level of discipleship grew out of their youth and students being given the opportunity to participate in overseas mission trips. Exposure to the needs of a lost world, and personally seeing how God was at work, created a passion in their lives that went beyond what in-house Bible studies and discipleship training had done in the past.

Within a few years several hundred members were participating in volunteer mission trips, and the church soon had adopted two additional Unreached People Groups. In the past, announcing a missionary speaker would have guaranteed low attendance, but now the annual Global Impact Celebration was the highlight of the church year. Members looked forward to renewed fellowship with their adopted missionaries and to hearing updates of what God was doing around the world.

But one of the most remarkable changes happened with regard to finances. Realizing the privilege they had to personally be involved in reaching the ends of the earth, Bob and others became burdened that they had not been able to raise their Cooperative Program allocation to previous levels and give even more to missions beyond their own budget needs. A decision was made to take 10 percent of whatever was given to their building fund and designate it to missions in order to maintain a more appropriate balance of giving priority to their Great Commission task.

The response was amazing. Within three years the building indebtedness had been paid off. Soon Cooperative Program giving had been elevated to 15 percent, with a commitment to increase it 1 percent a year over the next five years. In addition, the church was giving more than 300,000 dollars each year to its annual world mission offering which was dispersed to the Lottie Moon Christmas Offering® for International Missions, Annie Armstrong Easter Offering® for North American Missions and the state convention's mission offering and to help fund the church's direct missions efforts.

Although the story of Pastor Bob and Calvary Baptist Church is not an actual account of a specific church, it is a composite of a multitude of testimonies. It reflects what has occurred in churches that have caught a new vision of personalized involvement in their Great Commission task. I am grieved to find pastors who are so shortsighted and focused on the success of their local ministry that, they are depriving their people of the very thing that would stimulate growth and vitality within their congregation. Many tell me, following a missions emphasis, that they are focusing on strengthening their church programs, reaching their community, and paying off their building fund. After that they intend to get their church involved in missions. Seldom, however, does a church ever satisfactorily fulfill the criteria for moving on to another dimension of missions involvement, when it is seen as a sequential option.

But church after church that is challenged to give priority to international missions—providing opportunities for volunteer mission trips, encouraging generous and sacrificial giving to missions, praying for Unreached People Groups, and calling out missionaries—has found that they have been more effective in local growth and outreach. Oswald Smith, former pastor of the strong, mission-minded Peoples Church in Toronto, is credited with having said, "The light that shines the farthest, shines the brightest at home." If a church is involved in shining the light of the gospel to the ends of the earth, it is apparent that there would have to be a big, powerful fire of evangelism burning at home.

One church that has experienced a phenomenal increase in membership and baptisms marks the beginning of its growth at the point their members began to go on overseas mission trips. As each new family joins the church, they are encouraged to get a passport, because they will want to get involved in the exciting flow of mission projects around the world. At their current rate of increasing involvement in missions, the church envisions having a volunteer team somewhere overseas every week of the year. Every Sunday they will be praying for a team on the mission field and commissioning another group preparing to go!

Another church with less than 1,000 members has seen 72 career missionaries commissioned from its fellowship in the last 10 years. One pastor testified to the radical new dimension of stewardship among his congregation that has resulted from missions involvement by his congregation. He said, "When I became pastor 20 years ago, we struggled to give a thousand dollars a year to the Cooperative Program; now we are giving a thousand dollars a day! We have never had a problem meeting our local budget since we started giving priority to missions!"

COMMITMENT TO THE ACTS 1:8 CHALLENGE

The level of involvement a church reaches in international missions is usually multiplied many times over by its renewed commitment to mission work in North America and in its own state and community. Due to the lower cost and greater convenience of mobilizing people for ministries closer to home, churches that catch a vision for global missions are usually those most actively involved with their association, state convention, and in partnership with the North American Mission Board.

When the Southern Baptist Convention adopted the vision of "Empowering Kingdom Growth," it recognized that all we do should result in the expansion and growth of God's kingdom. The work of the denomination at every level is to serve and enable local churches for that purpose. Churches do not support the denomination so it can carry on kingdom work on their behalf; the denomination and its entities exist to support and facilitate local churches to be more effective in fulfilling their kingdom task.

The Acts 1:8 challenge is the practical way for local churches to implement the "Empowering Kingdom Growth" vision. Our Lord made it clear that the Great Commission was not a limited, localized focus of the missions task. We know that the "Go" in Matthew 28:19 is a participle that literally means "as you are going." In essence, wherever we happen to be, we are to make disciples . . . baptize and teach obedience. However, Jesus made the scope of our responsibility more explicit in Acts 1:8. He said that once we had received the power of the Holy Spirit we were to be His witnesses, "both in Jerusalem, and in all Judea and Samaria, and even to the remotest part of the earth." The "both" makes it clear that this was not to be a sequential process of evangelizing one entity before moving on to the other.

Immediately in the book of Acts we see God's Spirit bringing about a great harvest in Jerusalem. The witness of the apostles and others quickly expanded throughout the province of Judea, cross-culturally among the neighboring Samaritans and then to the Gentiles throughout the world. God has not given any church permission to draw a circle around its own community and say, "This is our mission; it is where we live and is the extent of our responsibility." The heart of God is for the whole world. If we are to be a kingdom people, and a church that exists to serve the kingdom of God, we will realize our mission task extends to all the people. We are responsible to reach those of different languages and cultures within our city; there is a shared responsibility with other churches to reach the unevangelized areas of our state and North America and also a role in reaching the nations and peoples of the world.

Our denomination probably did not have Acts 1:8 in mind in its earlier years in the nineteenth century when churches began to organize themselves into autonomous, local associations and later state conventions for cooperative work, mutual encouragement, and accountability. The Southern Baptist Convention was organized in 1845 specifically to bring together isolated and independent mission societies for cooperation in domestic and foreign missions. The result has been a voluntary structure of cooperation without any hierarchal connection or authoritative control over local churches to faithfully carry out God's kingdom mission.

Local associations are organized to enable the churches within them to reach their *Jerusalem* more effectively than what each of them could do working independently and alone. The state convention provides services to nurture and equip churches to be healthy and to facilitate their involvement beyond their community throughout *Judea*. The Southern Baptist Convention has organized the North American Mission Board to develop strategies and channel the involvement of churches in *Samaria*, with its megacities, ethnic population segments, unchurched counties, and underevangelized parts of the United States and Canada. And the International Mission Board enables churches to discover the blessing of direct, personalized involvement in fulfilling the Great Commission by reaching the *ends of the earth*.

Many churches have failed to grasp that kingdom growth is their responsibility, rather than the task of denomination and mission agencies. Even when acknowledging the scope of our missions task, it is usually seen as sequential. As one pastor explained it, "We are to reach our Jerusalem, *then* Judea, *then* Samaria, and *then* the ends of the earth." I replied emphatically that there was **no** *then* in the Scripture. We are commissioned to carry out the total kingdom task, and it is one that is to be implemented simultaneously. While we may agree with that perspective, the allocation of budget resources and the focus of our energies and programs reveal our priorities on Jerusalem and deny our perceived commitment to the Great Commission.

Yet churches are discovering a new passion for ministry and unprecedented involvement of members in missions as they embrace God's heart for the world and transform their church into a world-wide mission center. A pastor began to recognize that their worship and Bible study were to equip his people to witness and minister in the world. He said to his congregation, "We are no longer going to call our sanctuary our 'worship center;' it is our 'global outreach center.' God said in Psalm 46:10, 'Be still and know that I am God; I will be exalted among the [nations], I will be exalted in the earth' (KJV). The reason we gather to worship is to know God deeper and be equipped to exalt Him throughout the world."

A church that embraces Jesus' Acts 1:8 challenge must be intentional about engagement in the total task of God's mission. It must awaken its members to God's calling and cooperate with others to take the gospel to all peoples. There must be a conscious commitment to involvement in its community (Jerusalem), state (Judea), throughout the North American continent (Samaria), and the world (ends of the earth). Eight *Kingdom-Growing Responses* to this challenge have been identified as a practical guide for a local church to develop as an Acts 1:8 church under the leadership and power of the Holy Spirit:

1. **Prepare**—empowering a designated leader of missions and developing mission teams, strategies, and plans to take the gospel to our community, state, continent, and world.
2. **Learn**—bringing missions awareness and interaction to the

entire church body, training members for service, and connecting them to missionaries and mission needs.

3. PRAY—asking God for kingdom perspective and worldwide vision, interceding for Christian workers and unevangelized peoples.

4. GIVE—increasing the financial support of the Cooperative Program and other SBC cooperative missions.

5. GO—enabling a growing number of members to directly participate in short-term, long-term, and marketplace opportunities to minister and spread the gospel beyond church walls.

6. TELL—involving an increasing number of members in intentional, culturally relevant evangelism.

7. SEND—providing members with opportunities to hear and respond to God's call to vocational mission service.

8. MULTIPLY—participating in church planting, and facilitating church-planting movements.

Most churches are conscientious about their mission task but have been nurtured in a legacy of fulfilling their mission responsibility by supporting missionaries. About 70 percent of Southern Baptist churches participate in missions only through giving financial support to the Cooperative Program and mission offerings. They support the state convention and mission boards in what they do, but they have not envisioned any involvement beyond simply being a **supporting church**. However, many have discovered opportunities for involvement with missionaries and in strategies that reach beyond their local church programs. These **awakening churches** have taken initiative to sponsor occasional mission trips and volunteer projects for their members.

Others are **moving and growing churches** in missions involvement. A high priority is given to mission projects in these churches, not as a one-time experience, but as a continuing partnership with an overseas missionary or pioneer area of the United States. There is an increased utilization of media resources and information that enhances the knowledge and awareness of what God is doing around the world; an effort is made to mobilize widespread participation of members.

A significant number of churches are not just moving and growing with regard to awareness and participation in missions but have developed to the level of **strategic involvement**. These churches have partnered with missionaries and adopted people groups, or made a commitment to impact a city or area in another part of the country. They have aligned with IMB or NAMB field strategies to do whatever they can to see a city, people group, or population segment successfully evangelized and churches planted. Their people have embraced a mission lifestyle in their giving and sacrificial personal involvement in fulfilling the mission of the church. They exhibit a passionate commitment to intercessory prayer for their mission focus in the United States and overseas, and they maintain a consistent level of communication as partners with field missionaries.

A few churches have moved to a higher level of involvement to become **strategic mobilizers**. These are churches that have developed a sense of ownership and partnership with an area of the world, a strategic-focus city, or cluster of people groups. They have become an advocate for mission strategies among other churches. Sometimes referred to as "hub churches," they are taking responsibility, on behalf of the missionaries, to publish and disseminate advocacy materials, enlist other churches, and train and facilitate them to be involved in the missions task.

There is no clear delineation between these categories, but the point is that a church can plug into missions at any point. Wherever they are in their level of interest and commitment, their involvement can continue to grow. In fact, continuing development of participation in missions is inevitable. I have often likened volunteer mission trips to an advertisement for potato chips. The slogan of the ad was, "You can't eat just one!" Once members have been on a mission trip, seen the needs and how God can use them, they have to go back. The

Churches Reaching the Ends of the Earth

passion is contagious among the rest of the congregation, and participation grows into a sense of ownership for reaching a lost world.

Churches that have been engaged in evangelism crusades in Brazil or Romania begin to move beyond witnessing to planting churches. Those that have limited their overseas involvement to harvest fields have begun to catch a vision for the rest of the world and adopt Unreached People Groups. Others expand to focus on multiple people groups and soon have people going all over the world.

An amazing reverse impact in mission strategies occurs when a church begins to discover that the unevangelized people groups they are seeking to reach overseas actually live in their own city. A small church in Illinois adopted a people group in South Asia, then became aware that Asian Indians operated motels and worked in fast food restaurants in the vicinity of their church. They were startled to discover there was a sizeable community of their people group right there where they lived. Soon Bible studies were begun, and they found themselves a part of a global strategy without having to leave home.

Another church working with a nonresidential strategy coordinator to pray for access to an Iranian people group began to connect with an expatriate community of this people group residing in California. Representatives of most West African people groups can be found in New York City. Churches focusing on these peoples have been assets to the missionaries on the field as they have shared the gospel with those who are in the States. Most Unreached People Groups around the world live in places that are restricted, where it is difficult to proclaim the gospel openly. Practically all of them can be found in the United States where there is no restriction on witnessing. When churches have a vision for reaching them here, they find their relationships with families back in their home country become conduits for the flow of the gospel.

Beyond one's adopted people group, multitudes of international students, tourists, and immigrant workers from across the world are flooding the United States. Concern for security and terrorist threats have somewhat reduced the flow, but it is estimated that more than 600,000 students a year come from abroad to study in American colleges and universities. They are the brightest and the best. They will become the government and business leaders of the future and will influence society and the policies of their countries. It is tragic that they would spend four to six years in our country and never be invited to a church or have the opportunity to meet a Christian family. In almost every city are multitudes of foreigners who are lonely and desperate for friendship and encouragement. They are usually shunned by most Americans because of their strange dress and deficient language skills. We spend thousands of dollars to cover the cost of a brief volunteer mission trip to exotic places, but ignore the world that has come to our doorstep.

In the second chapter of Acts we read the account of Peter's sermon and the witness of the apostles on the Day of Pentecost. A number of ethnic people groups from around the world are listed; in fact, verse 5 says, "there were ... devout men, out of every nation under heaven," in Jerusalem, and they heard the gospel in their own language. Why should the disciples have been so amazed? Just a short time earlier Jesus had told them that they were to disciple the nations. It was as if Jesus were saying, "This is what I was talking about. I have brought them to you. I have demonstrated the power of the gospel to save them; now get with it! Go to the ends of the earth and be my witness to all peoples." Maybe we aren't going overseas in the numbers that we should, but God is bringing the world to us. A church that has a global vision will not neglect the peoples that God has brought within the shadow of their own church, in their Jerusalem, from the ends of the earth.

Commitment to a Kingdom Worldview

All of us view the world and life from the perspective of our own background and environment. Many of my friends in south Mississippi could not understand why I would be going to Indonesia years ago as a missionary when there were churches without pastors and so many unchurched people in our own community. For most people, their worldview is quite limited. It revolves around a small circle of family, neighbors, and co-workers and a fairly predictable daily schedule. We go to church and primarily relate to those with similar values, occasionally venturing outside our comfort zone to minister to the homeless, participate in a mission trip, or visit a new neighbor from a different region of the country. However, most of our conversation focuses on the familiar—the weather, family, the economy, and current sports events.

Television newscasts have exposed us to strange people and names of places such as Bosnia, Chechnya, Afghanistan, and Kosovo, but they are far away and have little meaning to our interests and lifestyle. What if we dared allow God to reshape or enlarge our worldview? Could we identify with those whose world has been torn apart by genocide and ethnic conflicts in Rwanda, Bosnia, the Congo, Gaza, and Dagestan? What would be our values and view of life if we were among the thousands of Christian people groups in the Moluccas of Indonesia, the tribal groups in Nigeria and the Sudan that were being massacred by Muslim fanatics? If our own country had the population density of India there would be 3 billion people in the United States. What would that do to our economy, health-care plans, and perspective on comforts and entitlements we have taken for granted? Floods, earthquakes, typhoons, and drought become more frequent and commonplace; they bring suffering and crisis to masses of people, paralyzing progress, and destroying hope of development among impoverished, developing countries. How would you view life if you were among the more than a billion Muslims locked into a fatalistic view of eternity or a Buddhist who saw one's destiny dependent on accumulating "karma" or good deeds?

Can you imagine what God's worldview must be as He, who created such a diversity of people and societies, views this spinning planet of more than 6 billion people? It would be a very simple worldview. He would see those who are fortunate enough to have been drawn into a redemptive relationship with Jesus Christ through repentance and faith. And then He would see the pain and suffering, the hunger and hopelessness, and the damning sin of the multitudes who are still separated from Him. If we are to be a kingdom people—a church that is committed to kingdom growth—we may need to reshape our worldview to see the world as God sees it.

Matthew 9:36 says, "And seeing the people, He felt compassion for them." A kingdom worldview would probably result in a reprioritization of our lives and stewardship of our resources. It would mean a commitment to pray specifically for the nations and peoples of the world. We would no longer focus our meager prayers on ourselves, our families, and those around us, but with broken hearts would intercede for those in darkness until the barriers crumble, the doors open, and the kingdom of God is extended. Prayer warriors would be mobilized, and the Spirit of God would move burdened hearts from praying to action.

Giving would take on a new dimension. Church members would no longer see it as their personal prerogative to determine how much they give of "their" money. They would recognize that having a secure job and steady income is because of God's blessings, and what they have belongs to Him. Gifts to missions would be a decision of faith, under the Lordship of Jesus Christ, trusting Him to provide for their own needs as they give above and beyond their means.

We are familiar with Ephesians 4:28 that says, "Let him who steals steal no longer; but rather let him labor, performing with his own hands what is good, in order that he may have something to share with him who has need." Obviously we would heed the exhortation not to steal, but let us not overlook the positive admonition. Why are we to work? It is not so that we can indulge in more consumer goods and attain a more comfortable lifestyle. We are to work in order to give to those in need. We may have thought of those in need as the homeless and less fortunate around us, but there is no greater need than those without the gospel.

1 John 3:17 says, "But whoever has the world's goods, and sees his brother in need and closes his heart against him, how does the love of God abide in him?" This probing question should convict those of us who have been blessed with this world's goods. Do we see the lost people groups still untouched by the gospel? Do we see the masses in bondage to superstition, following the futile path of false religions? Does our willingness to give generously and sacrificially reflect the love of God within us and give evidence that we have adopted His worldview? Do we understand that He has blessed us, like Abraham, to be a blessing to a lost world? But how can we expect families and church members to give more generously when the church allocates so little to those in need of the gospel?

A kingdom worldview will result in a church environment in which members are regularly hearing and responding to God's call. A pastor may not be able to make a passionate appeal for people to go to the mission field because he himself is unwilling to consider that possibility. However, if God has called one to a stateside ministry and confirmed His will for one to serve as a pastor and engage in a prophetic pulpit ministry, then God's kingdom purpose should be reflected in volunteers and missionary candidates offering their lives to missionary service. Kingdom churches will understand how to nurture candidates in getting the experience to qualify for appointment. They will guide them into appropriate categories of service and connect them with IMB personnel consultants who will partner with them and walk with them through the pilgrimage of determining God's will and place of service.

Obviously the majority of church members are not going to sense God's call to become missionaries. But that doesn't exempt them from involvement in God's kingdom task. Praying, giving, and participating in volunteer mission projects are something everyone can do. There are some who can contribute even more to reaching the ends of the earth. As the speed and convenience of transportation and communication grows, more and more business enterprises are becoming global. Commerce is no longer characterized by local or even national markets. Manufacturing components are produced all over the world. Developing countries are new players in the global economy and yearn for guidance and training. The door is open for consultants; multinational businesses have been the channel through which thousands of Southern Baptists have found themselves on overseas assignments.

It is estimated that as many as 24,000 Southern Baptists a year may travel just to China on business. Many isolate themselves with their American colleagues in an expatriate community, but "kingdom professionals" project themselves into the midst of the culture, building relationships with local clients and partners who need Christ. Their contacts with government officials and influential businessmen have helped create a better understanding of the Christian faith and have reduced hostilities and restrictions for local believers and missionaries.

A growing number of entrepreneurial "kingdom professionals" are opening branches or creating new business enterprises in countries to provide a platform for witness that would not otherwise be possible. Teams of doctors, educators, coaches, and business consultants have been welcomed in places closed to the gospel, because they can meet a need. They are welcomed, even as Christians, because the value of their services and expertise makes it worth the risk for a government struggling to catch up with the modern world. Many business and professional people in our churches are faithfully serving the Lord, giving generously and readily witnessing to others when an opportunity arises to share their faith, but they have never considered that their vocation and business could have a unique role in international missions.

God has blessed many among us and in our churches with profitable investments and significant wealth. Many of these people have moved into the latter years of life and are giving thought to the transfer of their assets. Are these decisions based on a kingdom perspective? My busy pace of travel is punctuated by occasional days in the office, which means wading through a pile of mail. Invariably there is a notification from a family, or state Baptist foundation, that a trust or portion of an estate from a deceased loved one has been allocated to the International Mission Board. While we are occasionally informed by those who name the IMB as a benefactor in their wills, most are a total surprise from people we have never known. Many dedicated Southern Baptists have become aware that their wealth can live beyond their own witness and influence here on earth to continue to extend the kingdom of God. Unless otherwise designated by the donor, gifts from these wills and trusts go into an endowment to assure the future of mission efforts to share the gospel around the world. Instead of being exhausted as a gift to a one-time need, these funds continue to multiply far beyond the initial investment to provide resources for global missions indefinitely.

While there has been tremendous progress in global evangelization, it is unlikely that the Great Commission will be completed in the lifetime of those who are a part of the older generation. Many will not live to see that day when the final people group is reached. But they can have a part in completing the task by setting up trusts, including the IMB in their wills, and providing kingdom resources that will outlive them. It is often said of our wealth that we cannot take it with us. How wonderful that it can continue to reap eternal dividends long after we have gone on to fellowship with our Lord Jesus Christ in heaven.

We are grateful for the faithfulness of Southern Baptists in giving to the Cooperative Program and the Lottie Moon Christmas Offering®, all of which is fully utilized in our budget of ministry and missionary support. But the potential of kingdom growth continuing until the Great Commission has been completed is enhanced by those who invest in future mission efforts. It is exciting to think about being among that great cloud of witnesses, watching the resources and material wealth with which God has blessed us in this lifetime, continue to be used to reach a lost world.

When my wife and I were married right out of college, our commitment to missions had already been solidified. Some of our friends jokingly said our passion for missions bordered on being obnoxious! We probably were a little condescending when we questioned whether or not one was really saved if they had never considered the possibility of missionary service. Nevertheless, there was no question of our calling and kingdom perspective when we had our Baptist Student Union choir sing "O Zion, Haste" as the recessional at our wedding. I will never forget going out of the church sanctuary together to the challenge of the refrain, *Publish glad tidings, tidings of peace, tidings of Jesus, redemption and release.* That was the purpose to which our marriage and our lives were devoted.

However, I never paid much attention to the words of that hymn until both of my children and their spouses, along with our grandchildren, were leaving for the mission field. The fourth verse suddenly took on a new meaning.

> *Give of thy sons to bear the message glorious;*
> *Give of thy wealth to speed them on their way;*
> *Pour out thy soul for them in prayer victorious;*
> *And all thou spendest Jesus will repay.*

It takes a special commitment for parents and family to give their children and grandchildren to the Lord, but we need to realize they belong to Him. What greater joy than to know God has chosen them for kingdom service to reach a lost world! It is a commitment to kingdom growth that will see men, women, and young people responding to the call to go. We will give generously to provide their support and pour out our soul in prayer that our Lord Jesus would be glorified to the ends of the earth.

Does empowering kingdom growth to the ends of the earth have anything to do with end times and the return of Christ? As we have already noted, Jesus said in Matthew 24:14, "this gospel of the kingdom shall be preached in the whole world as a testimony to all the nations, and then the end will come." My frequent reference to this verse has led some to presume that the second coming of Christ is the impetus for our mission efforts to get the gospel to all the world. Although I believe in the personal, bodily return of our Lord at anytime, I have never personally been concerned about the timing of that glorious event. God calls us to salvation, and we are simply to walk in faithfulness and obedience in the task to which He calls us as His people. In fact, Jesus said to His disciples when asked about the timing of His return in Acts 1:7-8, "It is not for you to know times or [seasons], which the Father has fixed by His own authority . . . but . . . you shall be My witnesses . . . even to the remotest part of the earth."

No one but the Father knows when the second coming will occur. That is not to be our concern, but our focus is to be proclaiming the gospel where we live and to the ends of the earth. Many people are interpreting contemporary global events into biblical prophecy and monitoring conflict in the Middle East to predict the end times. The signs of Christ's coming will continue to be prolific, creating speculation, but the one thing Jesus made clear is that global evangelization will precede the end.

I would never presume to predict the Father's time frame nor interpret His criteria for determining when the gospel has been preached to all peoples, but it is evident that we are living in an era when the words of Jesus are being fulfilled. There is no country on earth that has not been penetrated with a Christian witness. People groups who have never heard are systematically being touched by the gospel. Evangelism tools are being developed, missionaries are being deployed, and innovative strategies are being implemented in places that would have been unimaginable just a few years ago. Unprecedented progress is being made in giving all peoples an opportunity to hear, understand, and respond to the gospel. We don't work to advance the Father's timetable and to hasten the Lord's return, but to be obedient to the kingdom task to which He has called us.

Some interpret Matthew 24:14 in eschatological terms of fulfillment in the millennial reign of Christ rather than as a result of our mission efforts. Nevertheless, if it is the Father's desire to be exalted among the nations and His ultimate purpose is for every tribe, people, and language to be represented among the redeemed around His throne, then we should strive with all diligence to fulfill our Lord's command and make disciples of all nations.

For almost a decade IMB missionaries have been reporting an average of more than 1,000 baptisms a day as increasing numbers of new believers come to faith in Jesus Christ. An average of 170 new people groups have been reached with the gospel for the first time in each of the last three years as God is breaking down historic boundaries and opening doors of witness. He is mobilizing His people and moving in miraculous ways to extend His kingdom to the ends of the earth.

As I share testimonies and report on kingdom advance overseas, I am often asked why we don't see these kinds of things happening in America. Some will go on to reflect on questions that are not totally rhetorical: "Why are our churches plateaued and ineffective?" "Why is there such indifference and spiritual lethargy?" "In spite of prolific numbers of churches and our history of Christian witness, why do we seem to make little impact on society, why does our nation continue to slide morally, and why are Christian values diminishing in our country?"

I haven't had an answer to these questions and have personally been disturbed by the same observations. These conditions are not unexpected when we are confronted with the tragedy of those in spiritual darkness in other cultures where the gospel is not known, but what is the explanation in our own country? Upon examination of the Scripture, I have begun to gain some insight into a possible explanation. Israel had become God's chosen people, not because they deserved His favor, but so that they would be a people through which God could fulfill His mission. He blessed them, not for their benefit, but to be a priestly nation to be "a light of the nations so that My salvation may reach to the end of the earth" (Isaiah 49:6).

When Jesus gave the Great Commission to His followers, He was expressing and clarifying God's purpose for all nations to become His disciples. But did they get it? Did they move out in obedience to follow His purpose in carrying the gospel to Judea, cross-culturally to Samaria, and on to the ends of the earth? No, they stayed in Jerusalem until God had to allow persecution to come in order for the believers to be dispersed, carrying the gospel with them (Acts 8:1).

Throughout the Old Testament we read of God allowing Israel to be conquered and punished by pagan tribes. We usually observe it is because they forsook God to worship idols and other gods. But was not this, and the subsequent consequences, the result of their disobedience to fulfill God's purpose of glorifying Him among the nations? Instead of leading those around them to know God, they compromised and conformed to the cultural worldviews in which they lived. Instead of focusing on extending God's kingdom and proclaiming His glory among the nations, they became self-centered, concerned for their own welfare and blessings. Paul observes in Romans that the hearts of the Jews had become hardened and they were rejected "until the fullness of the Gentiles (the nations) has come in" (Romans 11:25). Israel was disobedient in following God because their eyes had become blind to God's purpose. They became self-centered, focusing on themselves and their special status instead of their mission to reach the nations. Their hearts were hardened toward God and toward the peoples in darkness to whom they were to be witnesses.

Could it be that God's blessings and anointing will be withheld until we regain a vision for our purpose as the people of God? To what extent must God allow our nation to suffer and our churches to flounder before we begin to look beyond our own programs and interests to our larger kingdom mission? If all the peoples of the world are to know Him, and God's kingdom is to be extended to the ends of the earth, it is up to us, the spiritual descendants of Abraham. May we not follow the example of Israel who became blind to God's purpose and whose hearts were hardened toward God and a lost world. Let us be obedient as His instruments for kingdom growth.

CONTACT INFORMATION

International Mission Board
3806 Monument Avenue
P.O. Box 6767
Richmond, Virginia 23230-0767

INTERNET HOME PAGE: http://imb.org
E-MAIL: imb@imb.org
ORDER RESOURCES: http://resources.imb.org

FOR INFORMATION, RESOURCES, AND ASSISTANCE
Get your church involved in international missions
Connect with a missionary or people group
Reach a staff member
Order resources
Support IMB missionaries and their ministries
Contribute to world hunger and relief ministries
Obtain general IMB information
Call (800) 999-3113

Volunteer missions opportunities
Internet: http://going.imb.org/vim
E-mail: imb@imb.org
Call: (800) 999-3113 (option 3)

Initial contact for missionary service
Internet: http://going.imb.org
E-mail: initial.contacts@imb.org
Call: (888) I CAN GO 1 (422-6461)

Prayer involvement
PrayerLine—24-hour missionary prayer requests
Call: (800) 395-PRAY (7729)

CompassionNet®—overseas prayer requests via the Internet:
http://imb.org/compassionnet

Especially for pastors and other leaders:

The Acts 1:8 Challenge
By registering for the Acts 1:8 Challenge, the
International Mission Board, North American Mission Board, cooperating Baptist state conventions and local Baptist associations will
assist you in designing and implementing a comprehensive
missions strategy specifically for your church.

To learn more, e-mail info@ActsOne8.com or
call (800) 4 ACTS 18 (422-8718).
To register, visit www.ActsOne8.com

CHURCH SERVICES TEAM

"Helping your church connect with God's global mission" is
the purpose and daily work of the IMB Church Services Team.
Pastors and church leaders will receive the encouragement,
coaching, and connections they need to lead their people to
effective missions involvement.
To find help, e-mail imb@imb.org or call (800) 999-3113.

ADOPT AN UNREACHED PEOPLE GROUP—
IMPACT ETERNITY

Impact Eternity is a five-week study to capture God's heart and
purpose for people groups around the world and how your
church can become involved. This study provides the
biblical foundation and the first steps in the process of
adopting an Unreached People Group.
Visit http://imb.org or call toll-free (800) 999-3113 for information.
Grand Rapids MI

SCRIPTURE REFERENCES

GLOSSARY

ACTS 1:8 CHALLENGE—Officially launched in May 2004, it is a call for Southern Baptist Convention churches to move to a new level of missions commitment by cooperating with their local Baptist association, their state convention, the North American Mission Board (NAMB), and International Mission Board (IMB) to take the gospel to their community (Jerusalem), region (Judea), continent (Samaria), and the world (ends of the earth).

AD2000 AND BEYOND/GCOWE—A global, informal network of Christian missionary agencies, denominations, churches, and individuals committed to world evangelism.

APPRENTICE MISSIONARY—An individual appointed for overseas service with the IMB who is assigned to a three-year term under the supervision and mentoring of an experienced missionary. Following the three-year term a missionary apprentice may be redesignated as a career missionary or missionary associate.

ASSOCIATE MISSIONARY—An individual appointed for a four-year renewable term of missionary service who may not meet the educational or age requirements for career service.

AWE CONFERENCES—A series of conferences sponsored by the IMB in follow-up to the AD2000 and Beyond Movement to stimulate engagement of Unreached People Groups resulting in church-planting movements. AWE stands for "Accelerating World Evangelization."

BAPTIST FAITH & MESSAGE—The statement of beliefs adopted by the Southern Baptist Convention in 1963 and revised in 1999 and 2000.

BOLD MISSION THRUST—A 25-year mandate launched in 1976 by the Southern Baptist Convention to unite all agencies in a massive effort of "bold mission"—an effort to take the gospel to every person on earth by the turn of the century.

CHRONOLOGICAL BIBLE STORYING—A method of evangelizing, discipling, and training a people group by relating to them, in a culturally suitable manner, the stories of the Bible from creation to redemption to the return of Christ.

CHURCH-PLANTING MOVEMENT—A rapid and multiplicative increase of indigenous churches planting churches within a given people group or population segment.

CONTEXTUALIZED ECCLESIOLOGY—Pertaining to the faith and practice of any congregation within its cultural context.

COOPERATIVE PROGRAM—A partnership of missions support launched in 1925 among individual Southern Baptists, churches, state conventions, and SBC entities. Southern Baptists support missions in their state, nation, and world by giving "through" (not "to") the Cooperative Program.

EMPOWERING KINGDOM GROWTH (EKG)—An initiative designed to call individual Southern Baptists to renew their passion for the Lord Jesus and the reign of His kingdom in their hearts, families, and churches from which God can forge a spiritual movement marked by holy living, sacrificial service, and global witness.

Ends of the Earth—The IMB's passion and vision to see the Great Commission fulfilled and the kingdom of God extended among all peoples.

Evangelical—An evangelical Christian is a person who believes that salvation is available only through belief in Jesus Christ, has personal faith and conversion with regeneration by the Holy Spirit, recognizes the inspired Word of God as the only basis for faith and Christian living, and is committed to biblical preaching and evangelism that brings others to faith in Jesus Christ.

Evangelical Fellowship of Mission Agencies (EFMA)—Founded in 1947 as a voluntary association of missions-focused entities committed to discipling the nations. Primary participants are the leadership of member agencies.

Foreign Mission Board (FMB)—The name of the International Mission Board until June 1997.

Girls in Action (GAs)—A Southern Baptist organization for girls in grades 1–6 that encourages them to learn about God's love, become aware of the needs of others, learn about the importance of prayer, and become active in missions.

Great Commission groups/Christians/agencies—Those who emphasize the missions understanding and perspective of evangelical Christians. It may be used to describe the missions viewpoint of agencies and other groups who are evangelical in faith and practice.

Human needs ministries—Since 1974, the IMB's Human Needs Office (now the World Hunger & Relief Ministries) has been assisting missionaries as they meet the needs of people throughout the world. Projects are designed to not only meet physical needs, but also to accelerate, enhance, and support evangelistic and church-planting field strategies.

INDIGENOUS—Generated from within or capable of originating from within the local context.

INTERNATIONAL MISSION BOARD—Formerly known as the Foreign Mission Board, the IMB is an entity of the Southern Baptist Convention. The board's basic role is to lead and facilitate the international missionary involvement of Southern Baptists in partnership with overseas Baptists and other Christians who are fulfilling the Great Commission.

IRON CURTAIN—A Western term referring to the boundary which symbolically, ideologically, and physically divided Europe into two separate areas from the end of World War II until the end of the Cold War, roughly 1945 to 1990.

INTERNATIONAL SERVICE CORPS (ISC)—A program started in 1990 to provide Southern Baptist singles, couples, and young families the opportunity to serve alongside career missionaries in two- to three-year assignments around the world.

JESUS FILM—A two-hour docudrama about the life of Christ based on the Gospel of Luke. The film, distributed by Campus Crusade for Christ, has been seen in every country of the world and translated into hundreds of languages since its initial release in 1979.

JOURNEYMAN—An international missions worker 30 years of age or younger, unmarried, with a college degree, employed for two years.

KOINONIA FELLOWSHIP—Being in agreement with one another, being united in purpose, and serving alongside each other.

LAST FRONTIER—Portion of the world's population, comprised of UNREACHED PEOPLE GROUPS (i.e. less than 2 percent evangelical Christian) with little or no access to the gospel, in which there have been no new evangelical church starts within the past two years.

LOTTIE MOON CHRISTMAS OFFERING (LMCO)—Southern Baptist churches collect the Lottie Moon Christmas Offering® for the sole purpose of supporting international missions. The offering is named for Charlotte Diggs Moon, who first suggested that Southern Baptists collect money at Christmas to support foreign missions. She was appointed a missionary herself in 1873 and served in China for 39 years.

MAN OF PEACE—A person in a people group who is receptive to the gospel and who can be used by a missionary to reach others in his group.

MASTERS PROGRAM—Designed for those 50 years of age or older who are available to make a two- or three-year commitment to serve overseas, utilizing the maturity, skills, and experience they have gained during their lifetime.

MISSION-FUGE (M-Fuge)—Launched in 1995, it offers missions and ministry opportunities for young people, grades 7 through college, within a camp context for those who want to participate in hands-on missions and faith-sharing opportunities.

NEW DIRECTIONS—A sharpened focus to position the IMB for maximum global evangelization as it entered the twenty-first century. The initiative later became known as "Strategic Directions for the 21st Century" (SD21).

ONESTORY—Formerly known as Epic Partners, this partnership provides churches with strategies and resources to use oral methods (Bible storying) in reaching the remaining Unreached People Groups. OneStory is a partnership between the International Mission Board, Youth With A Mission, Wycliffe and The Seed Company, and Campus Crusade for Christ.

PEOPLE GROUPS/ALL PEOPLES/ETHNOS—A group of individuals, frequently speaking the same language, who share a self-identity and worldview. Strategically, a people group is the largest group through which the gospel can flow without encountering a significant barrier.

PERSONALIZATION—A strategy implemented by the IMB to increase the involvement of churches and SBC partners in global missions. Goals include training missionaries to establish and nurture personalized relationships with churches and other partners; and training IMB staff to provide quality, personalized service to churches, state conventions, associations, and other SBC entities.

PLATFORM—The legal conditions under which a missionary resides within a country.

PRAYERPLUS—A partnership that links a church with an unengaged people group identified by overseas field leadership.

PRAYERWALKING—On-site intercession; walking and talking with God, hearing and heeding His voice, seeing and sensing as He does.

REAP (Rapid Entry Advance Plan)—Through this strategy, Southern Baptist churches, partnerships of churches, or associations have a unique opportunity to become missionaries to a people group in Peru, sharing the good news of Jesus Christ and planting churches.

ROPAL—An acronym for Registry of Peoples and Languages. The registry of Peoples and Languages was replaced in 2000 with two new registries—the Registry of Peoples (ROP) and Registry of Languages (ROL). The primary reason for the separation was the recognition that any given people group may speak several languages, and any given language may be spoken by more than one people group.

ROYAL AMBASSADORS (RAs)—Royal Ambassadors is a Bible-centered, church-based, Southern Baptist missions education organization for boys in grades 1-6.

SOUTHERN BAPTIST CONVENTION (SBC)—The nation's largest evangelical denomination, the SBC is an alliance of approximately 42,000 U.S. churches working in friendly cooperation under the heading "Southern Baptist." The Southern Baptist Convention, which refers to both the denomination and its annual meeting, has grown to more than 16 million members since its organization in 1845.

STRATEGY COORDINATOR—A missionary who takes responsibility for developing a comprehensive plan aimed at initiating and nurturing a church-planting movement among an Unreached People Group or population segment.

UNENGAGED PEOPLE GROUPS—Any people group without an evangelical church-planting methodology being implemented.

UNREACHED PEOPLE GROUPS—A people group comprised of less than 2 percent evangelical Christians.

VOLUNTEER—Used in reference to participants in the IMB's home office volunteer program and for overseas personnel serving four months or less.

WORLD CHANGERS—World Changers, which began in 1990, seeks to provide Christian youth and adults with opportunities to meet the physical and spiritual needs of others through practical learning experiences that teach servanthood and personal commitment to missions.

YOUTHLINK 2000—A Southern Baptist-sponsored millennial celebration for youth held in seven cities at the end of December 1999. The event involved young people meeting in arenas and conference centers to worship and listen to speakers and musical groups emphasizing the need to reach the world with the gospel.

WYCLIFFE INTERNATIONAL—Founded in 1942 by William Cameron Townsend, a missionary to Guatemala, Wycliffe works to translate Scripture, train field personnel in linguistics, and promote interest in translation.

INDEX

See also glossary of key terms, pages 213–220

Also Available!

$14.95

Lives Given, Not Taken:
21st Century Southern Baptist Martyrs
by Erich Bridges and Jerry Rankin

Lives Given, Not Taken: 21st Century Southern Baptist Martyrs is an intimate portrayal of ordinary people who followed God's voice. Written by Erich Bridges and Jerry Rankin, it is a book about danger, spiritual warfare, surrender, and sacrifice. But it also is about call, compassion, an enduring witness, and God's glory.

Order at **http://resources.imb.org** *or call (800) 999-3113.*

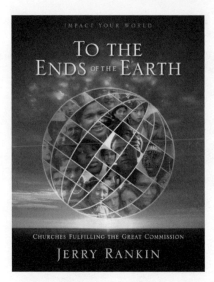

Impact Your World Series
To the Ends of the Earth:
Churches Fulfilling the Great Commission

Looking for ways to motivate your members to pray for, give to, and participate in missions? Here's all the impetus you need. This study gives church members, mission teams, and committees practical ideas for working alongside the International Mission Board and other channels to participate in reaching the nations for Christ. Filled with amazing stories of how God is at work in the world. To the Ends of the Earth offers practical ways for an individual, a church, or a team to strategize their missions involvement for maximum, life-changing impact . . . even in the farthest reaches of the globe. (9 sessions)

Impact Your World: To the Ends of the Earth Leader Kit
Includes DVD with video segments for each session. Segments include stunning footage of IMB missionaries serving in various locations around the world.
1415825831 * $99.95

Impact Your World: To the Ends of the Earth Member Book
Includes leader helps.
1415835322 * $12.95

Introducing ...

To the ends of the earth

a new mini magazine FREE from the International Mission Board

- Eight-page format for a quick read
- Up-to-date information on IMB strategies and missions advance
- Stories of God working through your missionaries
- Graphics, photography and brief articles
- Poster-quality center spread for bulletin boards and Sunday School rooms

FREE! Subscribe for yourself or in bulk for your church.

http://resources.imb.org • (800) 999-3113

"Acts 1:8 challenges every church to be involved in our Great Commission task at home and abroad. The IMB's task is to lead Southern Baptists to reach the ends of the earth. Help us share how God is at work by introducing others **To the Ends of the Earth** *mini mag."* —Jerry Rankin, IMB president

A Southern Baptist Convention entity supported by the Cooperative Program and the Lottie Moon Christmas Offering®.